# THE HOUSE OF MUHAMMAD

*The Sectarian Divide and the
Legacy About "Aya Tatheer"*

## Syed Abbas Rizvi

*AuthorHouse™*
*1663 Liberty Drive*
*Bloomington, IN 47403*
*www.authorhouse.com*
*Phone: 1 (800) 839-8640*

*Published by AuthorHouse  06/12/2019*

*ISBN: 978-1-7283-0751-0 (sc)*
*978-1-7283-0753-4 (hc)*
*978-1-7283-0752-7 (e)*

*Library of Congress Control Number: 2019904464*

*Print information available on the last page.*

authorHOUSE®

# DEDICATIONS

Syed Abbas Rizvi: This book is dedicated to Muhammad SAS the prophet of Islam, his Ahl al Bayt AS, and Janabe Fatimah Zehra, the beloved daughter of Muhammad, the prophet of Islam, who led a revolutionary movement for women's rights in the 7th century A.D.

## A Special Note from the Author

I submit apologetically to the almighty Allah for my myopic manifestation of reaching out to those who are unfamiliar with the truth with the hope that an impartial and unbiased approach would appeal to the intellectuals with optimistic foray. In so doing, I have reluctantly relied on a path for which I ask Allah for forgiveness. At the mention of the word Allah, Muslims automatically say *Subhanahu wa taalah (The most glorified, the most high)*. Similarly, before the mention of the names of Aadam (Adam), Ibrahim (Abraham), Musa (Moses), Eisa (Jesus), Muhammad, Ali, Hasan, Husayn, and the prophets mentioned in Quran, the preposition *hazrat* (your honor) is inserted, and after the name, *Aleha salaam* (peace be onto you) is recited. For females, as in the case of Fatimah the daughter of the prophet of Islam Muhammad, the preposition *Janabe* (exalted) is mentioned before her name, and *Salamullah aleha* (peace be on her) is recited after her name. I hope my actions are understood with the best of intentions for the sake of propagating the truth by taking such a course. I humbly request to all the believers to add the above prepositions and postpositional phrases as they come across these important names in the book.

# TABLE OF CONTENTS

# PREFACE

*I start this book with the greatest inspiration of my life, the words of the Quran.*

وَلاَ تَلْبِسُواْ الْحَقَّ بِالْبَاطِلِ وَتَكْتُمُواْ الْحَقَّ وَأَنتُمْ تَعْلَمُونَ

*And cover not Truth with falsehood, nor conceal the Truth when ye know (what it is). - 2:42* **(Y. Ali)**

Several years ago, I attended a conference entitled "Spirituality in Islam". Many renowned Muslim and non-Muslim scholars were presenting their views on the spirituality of Islam which has been gaining more attention in the non-Muslim world. In one of the presentations, a Muslim scholar casually began a discussion regarding a verse of Quran (Surah Ahzab, verse 33) where the purity of a group called the "Ahl al Bayt" is mentioned. The scholar then stated that this pure group, "Ahl al Bayt", was the wives of Prophet Muhammad. A non-Muslim scholar responded: "I disagree, 'Ahl al Bayt' was exclusively about Muhammad's daughter Fatimah, her two children Hassan and Husayn and her husband Ali.". The presentation ended, and the question answer session that followed evolved into an intense verbal brawl with both sides defending their cases. As it turns out, this was a part of the non-Muslim scholar's PhD thesis.

Recently, I had an encounter with another non-Muslim scholar of Abrahamic religions about this issue. Our conversation touched briefly on the significance of the term "Ahl al Bayt". He seemed to be intrigued by the term "Ahl al Bayt" and suggested that it would be of value if someone wrote a treatise on this topic.

I realized this suggestion was directed at me to take the initiative to investigate this highly debated part of a verse of Quran known as "Aya Tatheer" which starts with:

$$\text{إِنَّمَا يُرِيدُ اللَّهُ لِيُذْهِبَ عَنكُمُ الرِّجْسَ أَهْلَ الْبَيْتِ وَيُطَهِّرَكُمْ تَطْهِيرًا}$$

*"Innama Yuridu allahu Liyuzhiba ankumu al rigsa Ahl al Bayti wa yutahhirakum tatheeran".*

"Aya Tatheer" is the end sentence of the verse 33 of Surah e Ahzab. From here on, this part of the verse throughout the discussion will be referred to as "Aya Tatheer".

My goal was to examine all pertinent information I could from a wide array of sources, from Sunni to Shia, and non-Muslim as well. I wanted to examine the exegeses and expert opinions relating to the identity of the individuals referenced by the term "Ahl al Bayt" in verse 33 of Surah Ahzab. I sorted through thousands of pages of information from the dedicated works of experts on this subject.

Realizing the complexity in establishing the accuracy of information, I made my investigation procedures exhaustive and extensive. Since most of the information in this book is based on Quran, Hadith, Sunnah, Tafsir and history, I began to selectively focus on books, lectures, speeches, and discussions involving scholars who have an expertise in the interpretations of the Quran regarding this verse.

It was irresistible for me to pass on a task that I passionately believe can be resolved. I intend to walk the reader through the maze of information on "Aya Tatheer" while debunking false and misleading aspects to make the journey clearer. My goal is to make this an experience of learning, discovering and unraveling the myriad data to expose the incredible realities contained in this verse of Quran.

Finally, and most importantly, the Quran will be my basis to establish the truth.

# INTRODUCTION

أَوَلاَ يَعْلَمُونَ أَنَّ اللّهَ يَعْلَمُ مَا يُسِرُّونَ وَمَا يُعْلِنُونَ

*Know they not that Allah knoweth what they conceal and what they reveal? -*
*2:77* **(Y. Ali)**

The last part of verse 33 of chapter Al Ahzab is about a pure group of individuals recognized as the "Ahl al Bayt"; this part of the verse has become known as "Aya Tatheer". I grew up listening to this part of the verse all my life. The unique attribute of this verse is its focus on a selected group of individuals designated as absolutely "pure" by the divine will of non-other than Allah. Some contend "Aya Tatheer" refers to the wives of Prophet Muhammad, others contend that it refers to the wives and Muhammad's family of Ali, Fatimah, Hassan and Husayan, while a third group believes it refers only to the prophet's family of Ali, Fatimah, Hassan, and Husayn. This book will begin by discussing the strengths and weaknesses of Ahadith and exegeses of Quran regarding each of these three possibilities, then enter a discussion of syntax and grammar within the verse, and finally analyze all information presented to reach a conclusion as to whom the "Ahl al Bayt" in "Aya Tatheer" is referring to.

The term "Ahl al Bayt" is introduced in this verse specifically to serve a universal purpose. Interestingly, every scholar has taken the liberty to interpret it in his/her way to serve his/her specific agenda. As the partisan demands and needs grew with the passage of time, so did the views. This is one of the most deeply contested and debated verses of the Quran in past 1400 years and has led to religious divisions, deepening sectarian schisms, and conflict.

The identity and purity of these selected individuals are the main points of conflict. There are two controversial terms in this verse: First, there is the identity of the individuals referenced as "Ahl al Bayt"; Second, the term "wayutahhirakum tatheera" (loosely translated as: to purify you, a thorough purifying) which defines purity of these individuals in an exceptionally unique way in the Quran.

My preliminary search led me to identify certain features about "Aya Tatheer" that are unique and only used in this verse. The terms "Liyuzhiba" and "WaYutahhirakum" have been used only once in the entire Quran. Similarly the phrases "Yuridallah hu Liyuzhiba", "Ahl al Bayt wayutahhirakum Tatheera" and "yutahhirakum Tatheera" were also used only once in this context in the entire Quran. The term "Ahl al Bayt" has been used only twice in the entire Quran. This rare set up by Allah grew my excitement exponentially to further my exploration.

Predictably, experts have applied complicated interpretative methods of analyses as the political demands influenced their investigations. There is, in fact, a reasonably simple solution if clear Quranic guidelines are applied.

Since these discussions are based on tafaseer (exegesis of Quran) that are in some cases supported by Ahadith (traditions), Sunnah(praxis) and histories, it is crucial to touch briefly on the reliability of Ahadith, Sunnah and histories. Hadith and Sunnah are the actions and sayings of Muhammad. Since Ahadith, Sunnah and histories were compiled anywhere from 50 to 200 years after the death of Muhammad, uncertainties are created regarding the authenticity of the information from that period. Honesty, integrity, and reliability of the transmitters as well as the chain of narrators becomes a key factor.

One of the primary factors of concern about Ahadith is the period in which their compilations were composed. This was the period where two of the most despotic and repressive regimes known as the Umayyads and the Abbasids ruled. Their hostilities towards the daughter of Muhammad, Fatimah, his son-in-law Ali, and his grandsons Hasan and Husayn, are well documented. Muawiyah and his decedents abused Ali for more than seventy years. The annals of history illustrate the ruthless tactics that were used to terrorize Fatimah, Ali, Hasan and Husayn. Ali, Hasan and Husayn were assassinated under the dictatorship of the Umayyads.

An interesting fallout from the fall of the Umayyads was the rise of the Abbasids. The Abbasids opportunely seized power from the Umayyads to seek revenge for the massacre of the grandson of Muhammad, Husayn Ibn Ali, but instead began their own reign of terror against the progeny of Muhammad. Given these gruesome conditions, it is more than a miracle that the radiance emitted from the family of the prophet never seized to shine.

Muhammad had declared that Fatimah, Ali, Hasan and Husayn were an essential part of him. To hurt any one of them was the same as hurting Muhammad and Allah.[1] These members of the prophet's family all grew up under the care and guidance of Muhammad. Ideally, they would have been the most reliable and authentic sources for Ahadith and Sunnah. Unfortunately, many sources that provided Ahadith and Sunnah were not even close to Muhammad, and in some instances, were actively working against Muhammad's interests in the hopes of weakening Islam and undermining it for their own interests.

This purposefully misguided trail led to the developmental process of Ahadith, Sunnah and histories under the totalitarian regimes of the Umayyads and the Abbasids who, for 300 years, systematically manipulated facts and covered their actions with false Ahadith. Extortion, coercion, intimidation, massacres and murders were carried out to consolidate their power.

To challenge and establish the authenticity of a hadith or Sunnah, one must apply the process that Muhammad had declared as the Quranic test. The rule is simple: Accept a hadith or Sunnah if it agrees with the Quran; Otherwise, it must be rejected.

Unfortunately, it is surprisingly easy to mislead the opinions of people through the complex ways in which the Quran, hadith and history weave together to falsely identify the individuals they personally wish were represented by the term "Ahl al Bayt".

The terms "Ahl" and "Ahl Bayt" has been used in several verses of Quran. However, the term "Ahl al Bayt" as stated before has only been used twice in Quran. To deconvolute the complexities created by experts on the exegesis of the Quran, we need to study the conditions in which these interpretations were developed. The key to resolving this issue is dependent on the sincerity of the believer to use every opportunity to seek "Haqq" as defined by Quran. Haqq is one of the names of Allah. It is one of the attributes of Allah frequently declared throughout Quran. Haqq, generally translated as truth, is deep and multidimensional.

إِلَّا الَّذِينَ آمَنُوا وَعَمِلُوا الصَّالِحَاتِ وَتَوَاصَوْا بِالْحَقِّ وَتَوَاصَوْا بِالصَّبْرِ

*Illal lazina amanu wa amilu sualeyhate wa tawasau bil Haqqi wa tawasau bil sabri.*

*Save those who believe and do good works, and exhort one another to truth and exhort one another to endurance. – 103:3 (picktall).*

The above verse is urging the believer to Strive for justice and constitutional rights.

وَالْوَزْنُ يَوْمَئِذٍ الْحَقُّ فَمَن ثَقُلَتْ مَوَازِينُهُ فَأُولَئِكَ هُمُ الْمُفْلِحُونَ

*The balance that day will be true (to nicety): those whose scale (of good) will be heavy, will prosper: – 7:8 (Y. Ali)*

This verse provides assurance that justice (Haqq) will be served on the day of judgement. The philosophy of the term Haqq is complex and broad. According to the Quran, Allah is Haqq, Quran is Haqq, and Muhammad is Haqq.

فَذَلِكُمُ اللّهُ رَبُّكُمُ الْحَقُّ فَمَاذَا بَعْدَ الْحَقِّ إِلاَّ الضَّلَالُ فَأَنَّى تُصْرَفُونَ

*"seeing that He is God, your Sustainer, the Ultimate Truth? For, after the truth [has been forsaken], what is there [left] but error? How, then, can you lose sight of the truth?" - 10:32 (Asad).*

Since Allah is Haqq, everything he created must be perfectly balanced and in line with Haqq. Justice and fairness are only two components from the broad range of factors that make up Islam's social and moral structure.

Haqq is a major component of our discussion and is central to our truth-seeking mandate.

The purpose of life according to Islam is submission to Allah, the propagation of Islam, to implement freedom, love, and compassion, to respect one's fellow beings, to never bring compulsion in religion, and most importantly, to implement justice. Islam expects its followers (a true Muslim) to be role models for society. Honesty and truthfulness are demanded by Quran from its believers. Personal beliefs, opinions, theories and views in conflict with Quran have no place in Islam.

The integrity of the likes of Bukhari, Muslim, Tirmidhi, Faqruddin Razi, Zamaqshiri, and others must be carefully examined.

يَا أَيُّهَا النَّاسُ إِنَّ وَعْدَ اللَّهِ حَقٌّ فَلَا تَغُرَّنَّكُمُ الْحَيَاةُ الدُّنْيَا وَلَا يَغُرَّنَّكُم بِاللَّهِ الْغَرُورُ

*O mankind! Lo! the promise of Allah is true. So let not the life of the world beguile you and let not the (avowed) beguiler beguile you with regard to Allah. - 35:5 (Picktall)*

Unfortunately, experts are often driven by their own personal prejudices, either knowingly or unknowingly. Justice, the fundamental principle of Islam repeatedly stressed in Quran, is often ignored. The beauty of Islam is that the two cornerstones, "Justice" and "Tawheed" are intricately connected and inseparable. It is the responsibility of a believer to strive for Haqq and that he/she will be held accountable for any deviation from Haqq.

فَلَا تُطِعِ الْكَافِرِينَ وَجَاهِدْهُم بِهِ جِهَادًا كَبِيرًا

*So obey not the disbelievers but strive against them herewith with a great endeavor. - 25:52* **(Picktall)**

Allah, in the Quran, has declared that Muhammad does not say or do anything without the will of Allah. According to the Quran, only Muhammad has the absolute authority on Quran and Islam. Thus, to refute Muhammad's statement or actions is rejection of Tawheed. Whoever contradicts and disobeys Muhammad, according to the following verses, cannot remain a Muslim.

وَمَا يَنطِقُ عَنِ الْهَوَى

*And neither does he speak out of his own desire: 53:3* **(Asad)**

إِنْ هُوَ إِلَّا وَحْيٌ يُوحَى

*That [which he conveys to you] is but [a divine] inspiration with which he is being inspired. 53:4* **(Asad)**

وَالَّذِينَ آمَنُوا وَعَمِلُوا الصَّالِحَاتِ وَآمَنُوا بِمَا نُزِّلَ عَلَى مُحَمَّدٍ وَهُوَ الْحَقُّ مِن رَّبِّهِمْ كَفَّرَ عَنْهُمْ سَيِّئَاتِهِمْ وَأَصْلَحَ بَالَهُمْ

*But those who believe and work deeds of righteousness, and believe in the*

*(Revelation) sent down to Muhammad - for it is the Truth from their Lord,- He will*

*remove from them their ills and improve their condition. - 47:2 (Y. Ali)*

My approach will be to follow the principles charted in the above three verses, then utilize the Quran and present Ahadith that agree with Quran.

Although numerous books have been written on this verse, I have evaluated all the controversies and have discussed the most hotly contested aspects of this deeply debated verse. My goal is to present an unbiased approach that details the most referenced arguments, from which I will filter out the facts and provide clear conclusions on these seven verses (28-34) of Surah Ahzab.

Finally, it is the responsibility of those who seek the truth to pursue it, even if it is against those they admire.

Haqq or truth declared in the Quran has been set as our guideline:

*Illal lazina amanu wa amilu sualeyhate wa tawasau bil Haqq wa tawasau bil sabr.*

*Except for those who have believed and done righteous deeds and advised each other
to truth (Haqq) and advised each other to patience. (103:3; Translator; Yousuf Ali)*

وَلاَ تَلْبِسُواْ الْحَقَّ بِالْبَاطِلِ وَتَكْتُمُواْ الْحَقَّ وَأَنتُمْ تَعْلَمُونَ

*And cover not truth with falsehood, nor conceal the truth when ye know (what it is).
(Quran 2:42 Translation ; Y Ali).*

Chapter 1 presents verses 28 through 34 from Surah Ahzab. Translations and brief commentaries are offered about the verses surrounding the verse known as "Aya Tatheer".

There are three scenarios to be analyzed:

First, does the term "Ahl al Bayt" represent only the wives?

Second, does it include his wives and the family of Fatimah his daughter?

Third, is it exclusively about Muhammad, Fatimah, Ali, and their sons Hasan and Husayn?

These are discussed in chapters 3 and 4.

Chapter 5 provides analyses of the wording and gender modulations in "Aya Tatheer" to illustrate which individuals (between the wives of the prophet and the "Ahl al Bayt") are being addressed. The specifics of the gender change that takes place when the term "Ahl al Bayt" is used is also discussed in detail.

Chapter 6 is regarding the syntax and grammar of "Aya Tatheer", that goes into a thorough and unique process of analyzing each word of the verse. A final breakdown of each word is offered to examine the syntax and the semantics that lead to the most appropriate and accurate translation possible.

Chapter 7 addresses two important terms associated with the term "Ahl al Bayt". The terms "*Liyuzhiba*" and "*Wayutahhirakum Tatheera*" have been analyzed in depth because there are certain distinctions relating to these terms that play a key role in resolving the controversies. These discussions establish the specificity and the merit of these terms. Muhammad, in numerous ways, has declared who his "Ahl al Bayt" are. These terms as they appear can only be applied to this selected group identified by Muhammad, about whom Allah is taking the responsibility of creating as pure.

Finally, chapter 8 presents a comprehensive layout of the deductions and conclusions.

وَلَوْ أَنَّهُمْ آمَنُواْ واتَّقَوْا لَمَثُوبَةٌ مِّنْ عِندِ اللَّه خَيْرٌ لَّوْ كَانُواْ يَعْلَمُونَ

*If they had kept their Faith and guarded themselves from evil, far better had been the reward from their Lord, if they but knew! - 2:103* **(Y. Ali)**

أُوْلَـئِكَ هُمُ الْمُؤْمِنُونَ حَقًّا لَّهُمْ دَرَجَاتٌ عِندَ رَبِّهِمْ وَمَغْفِرَةٌ وَرِزْقٌ كَرِيمٌ

*Such in truth are the believers: they have grades of dignity with their Lord, and forgiveness, and generous sustenance: – 8:4* **(Y. Ali)**

### Verses 28 - 34

The interpretation of the six verses leading to "Aya Tatheer" is often seen through the prism of biases, vested interests, or oversimplification. The reality of these verses is both simplistic and nuanced. To approach them, we first need to reflect upon the seven verses, 28 to 34, of Surah Ahzab. These verses undoubtedly address the wives of the prophet of Islam, Muhammad. However, there is a sudden tonal shift that takes a specific group of individuals and raises them to an exemplary status characterized by the Quran as pure and flawless, known as "Ahl al Bayt". These verses will be presented and discussed with the purpose of creating a consensus from their varied translations. Relevant tafasir (exegeses and hermeneutics) of scholars on the subject will also be discussed in the following chapters.

These seven verses from Surah Ahzab (verses 28-34) were revealed in Medina, and the name Ahzab is translated as "Clans". The confederates had formed a coalition to attack Muhammad with the purpose of ending the religious and cultural movement he had started. This war was known as "Khandaq" (The Battle of the Trench) in which Muhammad was victorious despite the overwhelming numbers of the opposing forces. Ali led Mohammad's forces to victory by eliminating Amr Ibn Abduwad, a powerful leader and renowned warrior representing the confederates.

Various tafaseer (exegeses) suggests that these verses were revealed in response to the demands by Muhammad's wives for their shares of the spoils of war.

*Verse 28:*

يَا أَيُّهَا النَّبِيُّ قُل لِّأَزْوَاجِكَ إِن كُنتُنَّ تُرِدْنَ الْحَيَاةَ الدُّنْيَا وَزِينَتَهَا فَتَعَالَيْنَ أُمَتِّعْكُنَّ

وَأُسَرِّحْكُنَّ سَرَاحًا جَمِيلًا

> *O PROPHET! Say unto thy wives: "If you desire [but] the life of this world*
> *and its charms - well, then, I shall provide for you and release you in a becoming*
> *manner;(Translation-Asad)*

Islam has always established the greatest importance to free will and autonomy to its followers; the capability to choose one's own path be it within, or outside the system of Islam ("La Ikraha Fiddin" from Al-Baqara, verse 256 establishes that there is no compulsion in the faith of Islam). The Quran stresses a moral choice for the wives of Muhammad: The bounties of this world, or the bounties of Islam. With this option, they can choose this world's riches, and be separated from the Prophet, provided and cared for, and divorced in a "becoming manner".

Verse 29:

$$\text{وَإِن كُنتُنَّ تُرِدْنَ اللَّهَ وَرَسُولَهُ وَالدَّارَ الْآخِرَةَ فَإِنَّ اللَّهَ أَعَدَّ لِلْمُحْسِنَاتِ مِنكُنَّ}$$

$$\text{أَجْرًا عَظِيمًا}$$

*but if you desire God and His Apostle, and [thus the good of] the life in the hereafter,*
*then [know that], verily, for the doers of good among you God has readied a mighty*
*reward!" (Translation-Asad)*

Their second option allows them to stay and follow the path of Allah and Muhammad from which they benefit in this world and "the hereafter". The rewards in this world and the hereafter are only for those among his wives who are "doers of good".

Verse 30:

$$\text{يَا نِسَاء النَّبِيِّ مَن يَأْتِ مِنكُنَّ بِفَاحِشَةٍ مُّبَيِّنَةٍ يُضَاعَفْ لَهَا الْعَذَابُ ضِعْفَيْنِ}$$

$$\text{وَكَانَ ذَلِكَ عَلَى اللَّهِ يَسِيرًا}$$

*O wives of the Prophet! If any of you were to become guilty of manifestly immoral*
*conduct, double [that of other sinners] would be her suffering [in the hereafter]: for that*
*is indeed easy for God. (Translation-Asad)*

There is a distinct shift in tone here. Moral and ethical values become the central theme of the verse. This verse is specifically regarding the wives of Mohammad who are guilty of immoral behavior. The wives of the prophet of Islam were meant, to hold a higher responsibility, where they are viewed as ambassadors of the message of Islam. Morality is one of the main components of a believer and as the wives of the prophet, they are further accountable for any acts that may undermine the preaching's of Quran. The doubling of the punishment is emphasized because of the profound impact their immoral behavior may have on Islam.

Verse 31:

$$\text{وَمَن يَقْنُتْ مِنكُنَّ لِلَّهِ وَرَسُولِهِ وَتَعْمَلْ صَالِحًا نُّؤْتِهَا أَجْرَهَا مَرَّتَيْنِ وَأَعْتَدْنَا لَهَا}$$

$$\text{رِزْقًا كَرِيمًا}$$

*But if any of you devoutly obeys God and His Apostle and does good deeds, on her shall*
*We bestow her reward twice-over: for We shall have readied for her a most excellent*
*sustenance [in the life to come]. (Translation-Asad)*

This verse once again starts off with an "…if", making the opportunity provisional. Thus, those among the wives of Mohammad who obey Allah and his apostle and do virtuous deeds will have their rewards doubled. In addition to their obedience to Allah and the prophet, they are encouraged to embody the virtues of honesty, fairness, love, and compassion. Disobedience as stated in the following verse from Surah Nisa has been inserted to demonstrate consequential reprobation:

$$\text{وَمَن يَعْصِ اللَّهَ وَرَسُولَهُ وَيَتَعَدَّ حُدُودَهُ يُدْخِلْهُ نَارًا خَالِدًا فِيهَا وَلَهُ عَذَابٌ مُّهِينٌ}$$

*"And whoever rebels against God and His Apostle and transgresses His bounds, him will*
*He commit unto fire, therein to abide; and shameful suffering awaits him. 4:14 (Asad)".*

Verse 32:

$$\text{يَا نِسَاء النَّبِيِّ لَسْتُنَّ كَأَحَدٍ مِّنَ النِّسَاء إِنِ اتَّقَيْتُنَّ فَلَا تَخْضَعْنَ بِالْقَوْلِ فَيَطْمَعَ الَّذِي}$$

$$\text{فِي قَلْبِهِ مَرَضٌ وَقُلْنَ قَوْلًا مَّعْرُوفًا}$$

*O wives of the Prophet! You are not like any of the [other] women, provided that you remain [truly] conscious of God. Hence, be not over-soft in your speech, lest any whose heart is diseased should be moved to desire [you]: but, withal, speak in a kindly way.*

In this verse Allah is addressing Muhammad's wives as women of refined status. As wives of the prophet it was incumbent on them to present dignity, respect and a moral and ethical distinction. They are advised to recognize the importance of being representatives of a practicing and preaching Muslim. They are instructed to interact with others with kindness but at the same time be discreet and cognizant of any behavior that may be misinterpreted by people with evil intentions. Strong warnings to his wives for inadvertent "softness" in talk and flirtatious behavior is expressed.

Verse 33:

وَقَرْنَ فِي بُيُوتِكُنَّ وَلَا تَبَرَّجْنَ تَبَرُّجَ الْجَاهِلِيَّةِ الْأُولَى وَأَقِمْنَ الصَّلَاةَ وَآتِينَ

الزَّكَاةَ وَأَطِعْنَ اللَّهَ وَرَسُولَهُ إِنَّمَا يُرِيدُ اللَّهُ لِيُذْهِبَ عَنكُمُ الرِّجْسَ أَهْلَ

الْبَيْتِ وَيُطَهِّرَكُمْ تَطْهِيرًا

*And abide quietly in your homes, and do not flaunt your charms as they used to flaunt them in the old days of pagan ignorance; and be constant in prayer, and render the purifying dues, and pay heed unto God and His Apostle: for God only wants to remove from you all that might be loathsome, O you members of the [Prophet's] household, and to purify you to utmost purity. (Translation – Asad). (Note: The accuracy of the above translation is disputed and is the basis for writing this book).*

There are essentially two distinctly contrasting features locked in this verse. The first part is about the wives of the prophet. The prophet's wives are told to conduct themselves within the restrictions, integrity, honor, and compliance of the Islamic faith. The last sentence declared as "Aya Tatheer" starting with

"Innama …", in contrast to the first part, is about a selected group of individuals created as models by Allah and defined as pure to "the utmost purity".

This verse continues to address the wives of Muhammad to metaphorically "stay in their homes", thus advising them not to just manage the welfare of the family, but to maintain peace and to provide an environment that is conducive to support Muhammad in advancing the message of Islam to the community and mankind. They are discouraged from activities that are detrimental to the unity of the community. Stoking the fires of disruption, dissension and undermining the principles of brotherhood is dissuaded.

Moral ethical values mentioned in the previous verse 32 are reiterated. The words "tabarrujna" and "tabarrujna jahillia" reinforces respect and dignity. "Tabarrujna" in broad sense is to be coquettish or flirtatious. Conservative dressing and behavior are counseled. They are not to stoop down to show their charms as in the past characterized as a period of "Jahillia". The following tafsir explains the terms "Tabarruj" and "Jahilia":

> *In this verse two important words have been used, which must be understood for the proper understanding of its intention. They are tabarruj and jahiliyyat al-ula.*
>
> *The word tabarruj in Arabic means to become manifest and appear openly before others. The Arabs use the word baraj for every conspicuous and elevated object. A burj (tower) is so called because of its prominence and elevation. A sailing-boat is called barijah, because its sails become visible from a distance. The word tabarruj when used in respect of a woman will have three meanings: 1) that she should show the charms of her face and body before the people; 2) that she should display the adornments of her dress and ornaments before others; and 3) that she should make herself conspicuous by her gait and figure and coquetry. The same explanation of this word has been given by the leading lexicographers and commentators. Mujahid, Qatadah and Ibn Abi Nujaih say: "Tabarruj means to walk in a vain, alluring and coquettish manner." Muqatil says:*

*|It means a woman's displaying of her necklaces, ear-rings and bosom. "AI-Mubarrad*
*says: "That a woman should reveal her adornments which she should conceal. "Abu*
*'Ubaidah comments: "This that a woman should make herself conspicuous by display*
*of her body and dress to attract the attention of men". (Tafheem - Tafsir by Maududi)*

The discussion in this verse continues to be about the importance of prayer, compassion and adherence to the values of Islam. Basically, it is advising the wives to truly accept the values of Islam, learn and follow the code of conduct set by Allah and followed by Muhammad.

The key discussion and main argument of this book takes place in the transition of this verse beginning with "*innama* ....", where the tone of the verse shifts dramatically in introducing an elite group of individuals, "Ahl al Bayt", created as pure and faultless by the almighty Allah. These individuals were created specifically to be **placed among the community as models to be emulated** and Muhammad was assigned the task to introduce and recognize these selected personalities.

*Verse 34:*

وَاذْكُرْنَ مَا يُتْلَى فِي بُيُوتِكُنَّ مِنْ آيَاتِ اللَّهِ وَالْحِكْمَةِ إِنَّ اللَّهَ كَانَ لَطِيفًا خَبِيرًا

*And bear in mind all that is recited in your homes of God's messages and [His] wisdom:*
*for God is unfathomable [in His wisdom], all-aware. (Translation – Asad)*

In the last verse from this group of verses, Muhammad's wives are reminded of the sacredness of their homes. They are expected to practice and share the knowledge and wisdom they receive from Muhammad with the community and become proponents of the principles of Islam.

To recap, there are stark differences between these seven verses (28-34) and the "Aya Tatheer" section of verse 33. The first four verses 28-31 have statements starting with either "if you –" or "whosoever –" all directed at the wives of the prophet expressing the possibility of positive or negative outcome contingent upon their compliance to the proposed acts. However, in verse 32 caution is stepped up by advising them to guard against evils of their openness while interacting with community members with malice. Maintenance of respect and dignity is strongly instructed.

Verse 33 starts out by asking Muhammad's wives to stay in their homes, and to not behave as in the period of ignorance characterized in Quranic language as "Jahillia".

The clear contrast between "Aya Tatheer" and the verses before and after it becomes obvious as the tone swiftly changes towards progressive eminence directed only at "Ahl al Bayt" as models of excellence created and guaranteed by Allah for purity and flawlessness. Unlike in the previous verses 28 thru 33 there are no "if --" or "whosoever--" attached to the term "Ahl al Bayt". Absence of "ifs" and "whosoever" are some of the key differences between the other verses and "Aya Tatheer". It should be noted that "Aya tatheer" is free of warnings and punishments. The contrast between "Aya Tatheer" and the surrounding verses is considerable and will become evident from the discussions and analyses in the next few chapters.

Getting back to the last verse 34 of this set, the tone switches back to the style in the previous verses 28-33 as Quran stresses the importance of the wives displaying the utmost morality and dignity.

Muhammad's wives are anticipated to rise and maintain moral ethical cleanliness of the environment of their homes where verses of Quran are going to be revealed to Muhammad.

Verse 33 and the tonal shift that exists between the first half of the verse and the second, its meaning, and whom it is dedicated to is the main purpose of this book. First, a discussion on the term, "Ahl al Bayt" and its specific meaning is critical to understanding this shift and what "Aya Tatheer" means.

# Chapter 2

لِيُحِقَّ الْحَقَّ وَيُبْطِلَ الْبَاطِلَ وَلَوْ كَرِهَ الْمُجْرِمُونَ

*That He might justify Truth and prove Falsehood false, distasteful though it be to those in guilt. - 8:8 (Y. Ali)*

## Ahl, Ahl Bayt and Ahl al Bayt

The terms "Ahl", "Ahl Bayt" and "Ahl al Bayt" used in the Quran have a varied range of interpretations. Quran defines the physical relationships such as that of a son, daughter or a member of a family as "Ahl". The word "Ahl" is used in different contexts in Quran. "Ahl's" translation can be narrowed down to either "people" or "family" depending on which word it is associated with. The context in which the terms "Ahl", "Ahl Bayt" and "Ahl al Bayt" is used defines the addressee. In addition, this term expresses whether a person is qualified for receiving the honor of being an "Ahl" (part of a family or household).

An example is the verse of Quran about the son of prophet Nuh (Noah). Nuh's son is in a state of denial as the punishing rain starts to flood the earth. Nuh is pleading to his son to come on board of his ark and be saved, but his son continues to ignore his father's request and seeks higher ground in the hopes of surviving the wrath of Allah. The next two verses describe the exchange of communication between Nuh and Allah, establishing the basis to define what "Ahl" represents.

وَنَادَى نُوحٌ رَّبَّهُ فَقَالَ رَبِّ إِنَّ ابْنِي مِنْ أَهْلِي وَإِنَّ وَعْدَكَ الْحَقُّ وَأَنتَ أَحْكَمُ الْحَاكِمِينَ

*And Noah called out to his Sustainer, and said: "O my Sustainer! Verily, my son was of my family; and, verily, Thy promise always comes true, and Thou art the most just of all judges!" 11:45* **(Asad).**

قَالَ يَا نُوحُ إِنَّهُ لَيْسَ مِنْ أَهْلِكَ إِنَّهُ عَمَلٌ غَيْرُ صَالِحٍ فَلاَ تَسْأَلْنِ مَا لَيْسَ لَكَ بِهِ عِلْمٌ إِنِّي أَعِظُكَ أَن تَكُونَ مِنَ الْجَاهِلِينَ

*[God] answered: "O Noah, behold, he was not of thy family (Ahl), for, verily, he was in his conduct. And thou shalt not ask of Me anything whereof thou canst not have any knowledge: thus, behold, do I admonish thee lest thou become one of those who are unaware [of what is right]". 11:46* **(Asad)** _

The appeal to Allah by Nuh to show mercy on his son reveals the importance of the word "Ahl". Nuh, "Oh my sustainer verily my son is my 'Ahl' (family)", and Allah's response is, "Oh Nuh, behold **he was not of thy family (Ahl).**" Allah's outright rejection of Nuh's son being his "Ahl" defines the significance of what "Ahl" represents. The key factors for Nuh's son's disqualification as "Ahl" were his acts of disobeying his father, a Prophet and for being a disbeliever.

The following are further examples of the classification of worthiness of an "Ahl":

قَالُواْ يَا لُوطُ إِنَّا رُسُلُ رَبِّكَ لَن يَصِلُواْ إِلَيْكَ فَأَسْرِ بِأَهْلِكَ بِقِطْعٍ مِّنَ اللَّيْلِ وَلاَ

يَلْتَفِتْ مِنكُمْ أَحَدٌ إِلاَّ امْرَأَتَكَ إِنَّهُ مُصِيبُهَا مَا أَصَابَهُمْ إِنَّ مَوْعِدَهُمُ الصُّبْحُ أَلَيْسَ

الصُّبْحُ بِقَرِيبٍ

*[Whereupon the angels] said: "O Lot! Behold, we are messengers from thy Sustainer!*
*Never shall [thy enemies] attain to thee! Depart, then, with thy* **household** *(ahlika)*
*while it is yet night and let none of you look back; [and take with thee all thy family]*
*with the exception of thy wife: for, behold, that which is to befall these [people of Sodom]*
*shall befall her [as well]. Verily, their appointed time is the morning [and] is not the*
*morning nigh?" 11:81* **(Asad)**

This verse suggests that the daughters of prophet Lut (Lot) were also being referred as Ahl (Ahleka). His wife however is excluded from being an "Ahl" because of her association with the city of Sodom and her refusal in the prophetic mission. As such his wife is rejected from being Lut's "Ahl".

At-Tahrem (The Banning) –

ضَرَبَ اللَّهُ مَثَلًا لِّلَّذِينَ كَفَرُوا امْرَأَةَ نُوحٍ وَامْرَأَةَ لُوطٍ كَانَتَا تَحْتَ عَبْدَيْنِ مِنْ

عِبَادِنَا صَالِحَيْنِ فَخَانَتَاهُمَا فَلَمْ يُغْنِيَا عَنْهُمَا مِنَ اللَّهِ شَيْئًا وَقِيلَ ادْخُلَا النَّارَ مَعَ

الدَّاخِلِينَ

> *For those who are bent on denying the truth God has propounded a parable in [the stories of ] Noah's wife and Lot's wife: they were wedded to two of Our righteous servants, and each one betrayed her husband; and neither of the two [husbands] will be of any avail to these two women when they are told [on Judgment Day], "Enter the fire with all those [other sinners] who enter it!" 66:10* **(Asad)**

From these verses it is apparent that Nuh's, as well as Lut's, wives were rejected from being the "Ahl" because of their disobedience to Allah and the prophets. This demonstrates that being the wife of a prophet is no guarantee of being an "Ahl". This criterion applies to the wives of all prophets, including Muhammad.

وَ اسْتَبَقَا الْبَابَ وَقَدَّتْ قَمِيصَهُ مِن دُبُرٍ وَأَلْفَيَا سَيِّدَهَا لَدَى الْبَابِ قَالَتْ مَا جَزَاء مَنْ

أَرَادَ بِأَهْلِكَ سُوءًا إِلاَّ أَن يُسْجَنَ أَوْ عَذَابٌ أَلِيمٌ

> *And they both rushed to the door; and she [grasped and] rent his tunic from behind-and [lo!] they met her lord at the door! Said she: "What ought to be the punishment of one who had evil designs on [the virtue of ] thy wife - [what] but imprisonment or a [yet more] grievous chastisement?" 12:25* **(Asad)** _

The above verse defines the term "Ahl" or "Ahleka". It is about how Prophet Yusuf (Joseph) was being framed for an act he did not commit. It is not Allah but "Zuliqa" referring to herself as the family Ahl (Ahlika) of the Aziz.

وَحَرَّمْنَا عَلَيْهِ الْمَرَاضِعَ مِن قَبْلُ فَقَالَتْ هَلْ أَدُلُّكُمْ عَلَى أَهْلِ بَيْتٍ يَكْفُلُونَهُ لَكُمْ

وَهُمْ لَهُ نَاصِحُونَ

*nurses; and [when his sister came to know this,] she said: "Shall I guide you to a family (Ahl Bayt) that might rear him for you, and look after him with good will?" - 28:12 **(Asad)** ̲*

The above verse is a third example of Musa's (Moses) mother being described as "Ahl Bayt" by his sister who is recommending her mother as foster mother to feed Moses. Quran talks about Musa being rescued and adopted by the Pharaoh's wife Asiya. Asiya was searching for a foster mother acceptable to nurse Musa. His sister, posing as a bystander, suggests that she would identify "Ahl bayt" ("a household" meaning Musa's real mother) who would be suitable to nurse Musa. She mentions "Ahl Bayt" referring to Musa's mother. It is important to note the difference in the term "**Ahl Bayt**" in this verse and "**Ahl al Bayt**" used in "Aya Tatheer". It will become clear later why the syllable "**al**" plays a significant role in specifying which home is attributed to the term "Bayt".

Nuh's son, and Prophets Nuh's and Lut's wives were all excluded from being an "Ahl", but Lut's daughters were accepted to remain as his "Ahl". The term "Ahl Bayt" has also been discussed with the case of Musa's mother. The context in which these terms have been used defines the status of that person or a group of individuals. How these terms are culturally used are irrelevant. It only matters in what context these terms are used in Quran. The specificity is defined by Quran as seen in the cases presented. However, the term "Ahl al Bayt" has its own significance which will be presented as we drill deeper into its contextual characterization.

يَا أَيُّهَا الَّذِينَ آمَنُواْ لاَ تَخُونُواْ اللهَ وَالرَّسُولَ وَتَخُونُواْ أَمَانَاتِكُمْ وَأَنتُمْ تَعْلَمُونَ

*[Hence,] O you who have attained to faith, do not be false to God and the Apostle, and do not knowingly be false to the trust that has been reposed in you;- 8:27 (Asad) -*

### Does "Ahl al Bayt" refers to only the wives, or the wives and kin of Muhammad?

Some Islamic scholars quote the verse below about Allah granting Prophet Ibrahim's (Abraham's) wife a son. Sarah, his wife, is skeptical about conceiving a son at old age:

*They said: "Dost thou wonder at Allah's decree? The grace of Allah and His blessings on you, o ye people of the house (Ahl al Bayt)! for He is indeed worthy of all praise, full of all glory!" - 11:73 (Y. Ali)*

The term "Ahl al Bayt" was used addressing prophet Ibrahim's wife Sarah. Some scholars claim that since prophet Ibrahim's wife was addressed as "Ahl al Bayt", therefore, "Ahl al Bayt" in "Aya Tatheer" would similarly be about the wives of Muhammad. Superficially speaking, this assumption sounds reasonable. However, the differences between Prophet Ibrahim's wife Sarah and the wives of Prophet Muhammad cannot be ignored. Sarah was not only the wife of a prophet but also the mother of a prophet with blood lines stretching from the prophets Isaac all the way to Jesus.

The situation with the wives of Muhammad, in comparison to Prophet Ibrahim's wife Sarah, is different.

Two of Muhammad's wives were warned for misbehavior and threatened with divorce. Following are three verses relating to the response of the Quran for their unacceptable behavior:

> *When the Prophet disclosed a matter in confidence to one of his consorts, and she then divulged it (to another), and Allah made it known to him, he confirmed part thereof and repudiated a part. Then when he told her thereof, she said, "Who told thee this? "He said, "He told me Who knows and is well-acquainted (with all things)." - 66:3* **(Y. Ali)**

> *If ye two turn in repentance to Him, your hearts are indeed so inclined; But if ye back up each other against him, truly Allah is his Protector, and Gabriel, and (every) righteous one among those who believe, - and furthermore, the angels - will back (him) up. - 66:4* **(Y. Ali)**

> *It may be, if he divorced you (all), that Allah will give him in exchange consorts better than you, - who submit (their wills), who believe, who are devout, who turn to Allah in repentance, who worship (in humility), who travel (for Faith) and fast, - previously married or virgins. - 66:5* **(Y. Ali)**

When asked, Umar said that the two referred to in verse 66:4 were Aiysha and Hafsa.[1] The fact that they were threatened by Allah with the extreme measure of divorce suggests that the pasts of some of Muhammad's wives were not clean and pure. The second factor that creates difficulty in some of Muhammad's wives being within the "Ahl al Bayt" is that they never remained discernibly unblemished after the revelation of "Aya Tatheer". If they were a part of the declaration of Quran about their purity and integrity, they would not have been found guilty of breaking the tenets of Quran (33:33). Any disobedience to Allah's order would automatically disqualify them from being a part of "Ahl al Bayt" in "Aya Tatheer". The first example of one of the wives breaking these tenets is Aiysha, who, around twenty-three years after the revelation of "Aya Tatheer", staged a war known as "Jamal" which was responsible for thousands of deaths. The impact of this on the Islamic world was devastating. This was a violation forecasted by Quran at the beginning part of the verse containing "Aya tatheer" (verse 33 of surah Ahzab) starting with "And abide quietly in your homes". The Quran warned the wives of Muhammad from conducting any activity that would undermine the principles of Islam. Aiysha undermined Ali's Caliphate, and indirectly encouraged Muawiyah and others to revolt for power and turned a freely elected Islamic nation into a dictatorship and autocracy. Aiysha recognized her mistake and regretted profusely, so much so that according to Abul A'la Maududi, whenever she read the verse containing "Stay quietly in your homes", she would cry until her headscarf was soaked.[2]

It is important at this stage to discuss Muhammad's first wife, Khadija. Her distinction starts with being the only wife of Muhammad who gave birth to Fatima, who was the only daughter to provide Muhammad a lineage. Mohammad, about Khadija, stated she was among the four honored as "the leaders of the women in heaven". According to well-known traditions and most Muslim scholars, Asiya (wife of the Pharaoh), Mary (Mother of Jesus), Khadija (Wife of Muhammad), and Fatimah (Daughter of Muhammad) were "the leaders of the women in heaven".[3] Khadija was not alive at the time of the revelation of "Aya Tatheer".

Muhammad's wife Umm Salama is another example of a wife who aided and supported the prophet. She remained virtuous by playing an important role in propagating the message of Islam throughout her life. She was a witness to the revelation of "Aya Tatheer" but not part of the "Ahl al Bayt" in this verse, though he regarded her in high esteem.

Following Ahadith by Umm Salama and Ibn Abbas (cousin and companion of Muhammad) narrate that Muhammad declared who his "Ahl al Bayt" referenced in verse 33 of Surah Ahzab are:

Umm Salama:

Narrated on the authority of Umar Ibn Abi Salama, the son of Umm Salama, which is as follows:

"The verse *'Verily Allah intends to ... (33:33)'* was revealed to the Prophet (S) in the house of Umm Salama. Upon that, the Prophet gathered Fatimah, al-Hasan, and al-Husayn, and covered them with a cloak, and he also covered 'Ali who was behind him. Then the Prophet said: 'O' Allah! These are the Members of my House (Ahlul-Bayt). Keep them away from every impurity and purify them with a perfect purification.' Umm Salama (the wife of Prophet) asked: 'Am I also included among them O Apostle of Allah?' the Prophet replied: **You remain in your position** and you are toward a good ending'".[4]

Ibn Abbas narrated:

"We have witnessed the Messenger of God for nine months coming to the door of 'Ali, son of Abu Talib, at the time of each prayer and saying: 'Assalamu Alaykum Wa Rahmatullah Ahlul-Bayt (Peace and Mercy of God be upon you, O Members of the House). Certainly, God wants only to keep away all the evil from you, Members of the House, and purify you with a thorough purification.' He did this seven times a day".[5]

Some of the Sunni scholars consider that the term "Ahl al Bayt" is about the wives as well as Muhammad, Fatimah, Ali Hasan and Husayn. Maududi tries to justify including the wives of Muhammad as part of the "Ahl al Bayt". He attempts to quote ahadith to justify Aiysha to be included into the mantle of "Ahl e kisa" (people of Kisa). (See note 1).

Maududi's tafsir of this verse is as follows:

"But if somebody says that the word ahl al-bait has been used only for the wives and none else can be included in it, it will also be wrong. Not only this that the word 'household' includes all the members of a man's family, but the Holy Prophet has himself explained that this includes even himself. According to Ibn Abi Hatim, once when Hadrat `A'ishah was asked about Hadrat `Ali, she said, 'Do you ask me about the person who was among the most loved ones of the Holy Prophet and whose wife was the Holy Prophet's daughter and most beloved to him?' Then she related the event when the Holy Prophet had called Hadrat 'Ali and Fatimah and Hasan and Husayn (may Allah be pleased with them all) and covered them all with a sheet of cloth and prayed: 'O Allah, these are my household, remove uncleanness from them and make them pure. Hadrat 'A'ishah says, 'I said: I also am included among your household (i.e. I may also be covered under the sheet and prayed for)'. Thereupon the Holy Prophet replied, 'You stay out: you, of course, are already included'. **A great many Ahadith bearing on this subject have been related by traditionists like Muslim, Tirmidhi, Ahmad, Ibn Jarir, Hakim, Baihaqqi, etc. on the authority of Abu Said Khudri, Hadrat 'A'ishah, Hadrat Anas, Hadrat Umm Salamah, Hadrat Wathilah bin Aqsa' and some other Companions, which show that the Holy Prophet declared Hadrat 'Ali and Fatimah and their two sons as his ahl al-bait.** Therefore, the view of those who exclude them from the ahl al-bait is not correct".[6]

As stated in the above tafseer, Aiysha's eagerness to enter the "kisa" and Muhammad's out right denial when he said; **"You stay out"** followed by "of course you are already included" demonstrates Maududi's inability to definitively include Aiysha from the following discussion:

It would be necessary at this stage to analyze this Hadith and the following Hadith of Um Salam quoted by Maududi in a pragmatic way;

"Hadrat 'A'ishah says, 'I said: I also am included among your household (i.e. I may also be covered under the sheet and prayed for)'.

Thereupon the Holy Prophet replied, 'You stay out: you, of course, are already included'".

The statement by Muhammad, "You stay out", essentially stopped Aiysha from entering the cover of the sheet (Kisa). It is significant to understand and accept the fact that Aiysha was kept out of the cover of "kisa" while the verse was delivered inside the mantle of "kisa" in her absence.

The simple response by Muhammad would have been to let her in without saying "you stay out". Muhammad's immediate reaction to tell her to **"You stay out"** is an outright rejection from allowing her to enter "kisa". It is obvious that Muhammad did not consider her as a part of "Ahl e Kisa" or "Ahl al Bayt" in this verse. The extension, "you, of course, are already included" appears to provide a soft landing after rejection or an excuse to keep her out. The bottom-line is that Aiysha was not allowed to enter the "Kisa" where the "Aya Tatheer" descended on "Ahl al Bayt". The event of Kisa happened several times.

Maududi:

> "We have one authentic narration from the Mother of believers `Aisha (ra) in Sahih Muslim in which she says that Allah's Apostle SAWS went out one morning wearing a striped cloak of the black camel's hair.
>
> And where did he go? He went to Umm Salama's (ra) house and these verses were revealed in her house as she states in the authentic narrations:
>
> **Translation:** Umm Salmah (ra) said: 'In my house these verses were revealed '*Allah only wills to remove what is foul from you Ahlul-Bayt and to purify you thoroughly.*' So, the Prophet SAWS called for `Ali and Fatimah and Hasan and Husein and then said: 'These are my Ahlul-Bayt', In the Hadith of al Qadi and al Summi he said: 'They are my Ahel'. So, I said: 'O Messenger of Allah! aren't I also from your Ahlul-Bayt?' He said: 'Yes you are Insha-Allah'".

Muhaddith: Al Hakim from al Sunan al kubrah for Bayhaqqi:

> *"Hadith rank: Isnad SAHIH narrators all trustworthy. And there are different versions*
> *of this narration, in one he SAWS says to her 'Yes you are insha-Allah' and in another*
> *'You are upon goodness. (twice)' and some other versions…"*

The above Ahadith quoted by Maududi are variations of the Kisa event.[6] None of these Ahadith substantiate the claim that Um Salam was part of "Ahl al Bayt" in this verse. The fact is that Um Salama did not even ask for permission to enter the Kisa. She asked Muhammad if she could be a part of his "Ahl al Bayt" who were in the "Kisa". Not allowing Um Salama to enter the "Kisa" and saying "Yes you are inshallah" or "yes you are If Allah wills it" provides uncertainty. It is a mistake to presume that Umm Salama was specifically accepted as part of "Ahl al Bayt" under the mantle of Kisa. All Ahadith about Umm Salama suggest that she was respectfully kept out of the Kisa event.

The following are four responses by Muhammad from at least four different traditions about Um Salam's request to enter the "Kisa" or be part of "Ahl al Bayt" where the "Aya Tatheer" was to be revealed:

1. "you have a good future and you are one of the wives of the Prophet".

2. Um Salama, "I swear by the almighty that the holy Prophet did not grant me any distinction and said: "You have a good future".

3. "You have a good future but only these are the members of my family. O Lord! The members of my family (i.e. Fatimah, Ali, Hasan and Husayn) are more deserving".

4. "Allah will reward you and recompense you".
   Umm Salama, "I wished that he might have said 'Yes' and would have valued such a reply much more than anything else in the world".[7]

It is made clear by this point that Muhammad never allowed any of his wives to enter the Kisa (mantle). It was exclusively the privilege of Fatimah, Ali, Hasan and Husayn to be under the Kisa with Muhammad when Jebrail (Gabrial) entered the kisa to deliver the "Aya Tatheer".

An obvious and important fact is that Um Salama and Aiysha asked permission to enter "Kisa" or be part of "Ahl al Bayt" after the "Aya Tatheer" had already been revealed under the "Kisa" mantle in their absence. It was therefore impossible to include them in "Kisa" after the event had already occurred. The timing and the conditions in which the verse was delivered prohibited the wives from being a part of "Aya Tatheer".

The attempts by some exegetes to try and undermine the eminence of the "Ahl al Bayt" is troubling. An example is the exegeses of this verse by Ibn Kathir who quotes a hadith by Ikramah, a slave of Ibn Abbas who claimed that he heard from Ibn Abbas that "Ahl al Bayt" in "Aya Tatheer" was only about the wives of Muhammad.

It is interesting that in the same exegeses, Ibn Kathir quotes a hadith by Aiysha that contradicts Ikramah's hadith.

According to Aiysha:

> One day the Prophet (S) came out afternoon wearing a black cloak (upper garment or gown; long coat), then al-Hasan Ibn 'Ali came, and the Prophet accommodated him under the cloak, then al-Husayn came and entered the cloak, then Fatimah came, and the Prophet entered her under the cloak, then 'Ali came, and the Prophet entered him to the cloak as well. Then the Prophet recited: "Verily Allah intends to keep off from you every kind of uncleanness O' People of the House (Ahlul-Bayt), and purify you a perfect purification.

There is clear contradiction between Ikrama's statement and that of Aiysha.[8]

There are five glaring issues with Ikrama's hadith:

1. The foremost flaw in Ikrama's hadith is that it conflicts with Muhammad which, on its own, is enough to reject it.

2. Ikrama claimed that he heard from Ibn Abbas that the term "Ahl al Bayt" in verse 33 of Surah Ahzab was about Muhammad's wives, which contradicts Ibn Abbas's own hadith (shown earlier).

3. Ibn Abbas states that Muhammad had repeatedly indicated that Muhammad's "Ahl al Bayt" are Fatimah, Ali, Hasan and Husayn.

4. The tafsir of Ibn Kathir quotes both Aiysha's and Ikrama's Ahadith contradicting each other.

5. An important fact is that Ikrama was a Khawarijit.[9] He had the motive to undermine Ali and his family in any way possible.

There is also a hadith of Muhammad reported in the tafsir of Ibn Kathir related by Zayd under aya 33 of Surah Ahzab as follows:

> *Thereafter! O people, I am merely a human being and soon the messenger of my Lord will come, and I will answer him. I am leaving behind two things with you, the first of which is the Book of Allah in which is guidance and light, so seize the Book of Allah and hold fast to it.) He urged them to cling to the Book of Allah, then he said: (Thereafter! O people, I am merely a human being and soon the messenger of my Lord will come, and I will answer him. I am leaving behind two things with you, the first of which is the Book of Allah in which is guidance and light, so seize the Book of Allah and hold fast to it.) He urged them to cling to the Book of Allah, then he said:*

*(And the members of my family (Ahl Al-Bayt): Remember Allah with regard to the members of my family, remember Allah with regard to the members of my family.) saying it three times.' Husayn said to him, `Who are the members of his family (Ahl Al-Bayt), O Zayd Are not his wives' members of his family' He said, `His wives are members of his family, but the members of his family are those who are not permitted to receive charity after he died.' He said, `Who are they' He said, `They are the family of `Ali, the family of `Aqil, the family of Ja`far and the family of `Abbas, may Allah be pleased with them.' He said, `Were all of these forbidden to receive charity after his death' He said, `Yes.'" This Commentary is from Zayd bin Arqam and is not Marfu`(Marfu describes an act or deed of Prophet Muhammad).*

The above hadith about the wives of Muhammad and the extended family of Aquil, Jafar and Abbas has been characterized by Zayed as the family of Muhammad. It is interesting that it is Zayd who is defining the members of Muhammad's family, which is not consistent with how Muhammad himself has defined his "Ahl al Bayt". The identity of "Ahl al Bayt" will become evident as the next few chapters drill deeper into its context.

History, Ahadith, and Sunnah confirm that the term "Ahl al Bayt" in this verse represents Muhammad, Fatimah, Ali, Hasan and Husayn. What "Ahl al Bayt" represents in Arab society or any society is irrelevant here. It does not matter how anyone defines "Ahl al Bayt". What matters the most is how Muhammad defined his "Ahl al Bayt".

وَمَن يَعْصِ اللّهَ وَرَسُولَهُ وَيَتَعَدَّ حُدُودَهُ يُدْخِلْهُ نَارًا خَالِدًا فِيهَا وَلَهُ عَذَابٌ مُّهِينٌ

*But those who disobey Allah and His Messenger and transgress His limits will be admitted to a Fire, to abide therein: And they shall have a humiliating punishment. - 4:14* **(Y. Ali)**

# Chapter 4

يَخْتَصُّ بِرَحْمَتِهِ مَن يَشَاء وَاللّهُ ذُو الْفَضْلِ الْعَظِيمِ

*He selecteth for His mercy whom He will. Allah is of infinite bounty. - 3:74* **(Picktall)**

## Are "Ahl al Bayt" Muhammad, Fatimah, Ali, Hasan and Husayn?

At this point, we reach the last possibility of the "Ahl al Bayt" being only Muhammad, Fatimah, Ali, Hasan and Husayn. Rather than concluding simply based on a process of elimination, it is important to illustrate that there are many Ahadith, Sunnah, and History that provide a great deal of evidence and support to the possibility that the "Ahl al Bayt" are none other than Muhammad, Fatimah, Ali, Hasan and Husayn.

As we have already seen, there are quite a few Ahadith from Muhammad's wives Umm Salama, and Aiysha, discussed in previous chapters. They are repeated briefly to reiterate that the wives of Muhammad who were present to witness the event of the delivery of "Aya Tatheer" prove that Muhammad gathered only Fatimah, Ali, Hassan, and Husayn under the cover of the sheet with him when the verse was revealed to him. These are followed by the hadith of Muhammad's wife Saffiya and several Ahadith from his companions and relatives declaring at crucial moments who his "Ahl al Bayt" are.

Umm Salama:

"Narrated on the authority of Umar Ibn Abi Salama, the son of Umm Salama, which is as follows:

The verse

***'Verily Allah intends to ... (33:33)'***

was revealed to the Prophet (S) in the house of Umm Salama. Upon that, the Prophet gathered Fatimah, al-Hasan, and al-Husayn, and covered them with a cloak, and he also covered 'Ali who was behind him. Then the Prophet said: 'O' Allah! These are the Members of my House (Ahlul-Bayt). Keep them away from every impurity and purify them with a perfect purification.' Umm Salama (the wife of Prophet) asked: 'Am I also included among them O Apostle of Allah?' The Prophet replied: **You remain in your position** and you are toward a good ending'".[1]

The following are three different exchange of dialogues about the same event:

1.  "Umm Salama said: 'O Prophet of Allah! Am I not one of the members of your family?' The Holy Prophet replied: 'You have a good future but only these are the members of my family. O Lord! The members of my family are more deserving'."[2]

2.  "Umm Salama said to the Holy Prophet: 'Am I also one of them?' He replied: 'No. You have your own special position and your future is good'". [3,4]

3.  "Umm Salama: I said, 'O Prophet of Allah! Am I not also one of your Ahlul-Bayt?' I swear by the Almighty that the Holy Prophet did NOT grant me any distinction and said: 'You have a good future'." [5]

Safiyya:

"Safiyya wife of the Prophet (S). Ja'far Ibn Abi Talib narrated:

When the Messenger of Allah noticed that a blessing from Allah was to descent, he told Safiyya (one of his wives): 'Call for me! Call for me!' Safiyya said: 'Call who, O the Messenger of Allah?' He said: 'Call for me my Ahlul-Bayt who are 'Ali, Fatimah, al-Hasan, and al-Husayn'. Thus, we sent for them and they came to him.

Then the Prophet (S) spread his cloak over them and raised his hand (toward sky) saying: 'O Allah! These are my family (Aalee), so bless Muhammad and the family (Aal) of Muhammad' and Allah, to whom belong Might and Majesty, revealed: 'Verily Allah intends to keep off from you every kind of uncleanness O' People of the House (Ahlul-Bayt), and purify you a thorough purification (Qur'an, the last sentence of Verse 33:33)'". [6,7,8]

Aiysha:

"Narrated by Aiysha wife of Muhammad:

One day the Prophet (S) came out afternoon wearing a black cloak (upper garment or gown; long coat), then al-Hasan Ibn 'Ali came and the Prophet accommodated him under the cloak, then al-Husayn came and entered the cloak, then Fatimah came and the Prophet entered her under the cloak, then 'Ali came and the Prophet entered him to the cloak as well. Then the Prophet recited: 'Verily Allah intends to keep off from you every kind of uncleanness O' People of the House (Ahlul-Bayt), and purify you a perfect purification (the last sentence of Verse 33:33)'". [9]

Furthermore, following Ahadith by the companions and close relatives of Muhammad confirm that Muhammad has repeatedly identified who his "Ahl al Bayt" are:

Anas Ibn Malik narrated [10]:

> "The Messenger of Allah (S), from the time the revelation of 'Verily Allah intends to... (the last part of Verse 33:33)' and for six months thereafter, stood by the door of the House of Fatimah and said: 'Time for Prayer Ahlul-Bayt; No doubt! Allah wished to remove all abomination from you and make you pure and spotless'".

Abu al-Hamra narrated [11]:

> "The Messenger of God continued eight months in Medina, coming to the door of 'Ali at every morning prayer, putting his two hands on the two sides of the door and exclaiming: 'Assalat! Assalat! (prayer! prayer!) Certainly, God ward off all uncleanness from you, O Members of the House of Muhammad, and to make you pure and spotless'".

Ibn Abbas (ra) narrated [12]:

> "We have witnessed the Messenger of God for nine months coming to the door of 'Ali, son of Abu Talib, at the time of each prayer and saying: 'Assalamu Alaykum Wa Rahmatullah Ahlul-Bayt (Peace and Mercy of God be upon you, O Members of the House). Certainly, God wants only to keep away all the evil from you, Members of the House, and purify you with a thorough purification'. He did this seven times a day".

Abu Said Khudri [13]:

"For forty days the Holy Prophet approached the house of Fatimah al-Zahra (sa) every morning and used to say: 'Peace be upon you O people of the House! The time for the prayers has come'. And thereafter he used to recite this verse: 'O people of the Prophet's House....' And then said: 'I am in a state of war with him who fights with you and am in a state of peace with him who is at peace with you'".

Sa'd Ibn Abi Waqqas [14]:

"At the time of the revelation of the verse, the Holy Prophet called 'Ali along with his two sons and Fatimah and accommodated them under his own cloak and said: 'O Lord! These are the members of my family'".

Abu Sa'id al-Khudri [15]:

"I heard the Messenger of Allah saying: 'This verse has been revealed about five individuals: Myself, 'Ali, al-Hasan, al-Husayn, and Fatimah'".

Wathilah Ibn Asqa [16]:

"I was sitting with Wathilah Ibn Asqa' when a discussion took place about 'Ali and the people abused him. When those present, rose to leave he said to me: 'Keep sitting so that I may talk with you about the man whom they have been abusing. I was with the Holy Prophet when 'Ali, Fatimah, al-Hasan and al-Husayn approached him and the Holy Prophet spread his cloak on them and said: 'O Allah! These are the members of my family. Ward off every uncleanness from them and keep them clean and pure.'"

Shaddad Ibn Abdullah [17]:

"I heard from Wathilah Ibn Asqa' that when the head of (Imam) al-Husayn was brought, one of the Syrians abused (Imam) al-Husayn and his father, Wathilah stood up and said: 'I swear by Allah that ever since I heard the Holy Prophet say about them: 'O People of the Prophet's House! Allah intends to keep you pure from uncleanness and blemish and to purify you with a thorough purification,' I have always loved 'Ali, Fatimah, al-Hasan and al-Husayn (Peace be upon them)'".

These include those of Tirmidhi ("*Sahih*" 166/2) which quotes S`ad ibn Abi Waqqas as follows: "*When the mubahalah verse was recited, the Holy Prophet (S) summoned `Ali, Fatimah, Hasan, and Husayn and said: `O Allah, these are the Members of my Household*".

Ibrahim Al Qunduzi in "Yanabi al Mawaddah", states that in "Aya Tatheer", the term "Ahl al Bayt" is only regarding Muhammad, Ali, Fatimah, Hasan and Husayn [18].

In addition to the Ahadith originally presented, there are many other verses and events reinforcing Muhammad's declaration of who his "Ahl al Bayt" are. The three renowned historic events widely referenced as Mubahala, Aya Mawaddah, and Ghadir e Khumm serve to further clarify the individuals who can make up the "Ahl al Bayt".

**Mubahala:**

The event known as Mubahala began when the Christians from Najran came to ask Muhammad about the Islamic view regarding Jesus. Muhammad asked them to come back the following day for an answer. The following three verses were revealed in response to their enquiry about Jesus in the Quran:

إِنَّ مَثَلَ عِيسَى عِندَ اللّهِ كَمَثَلِ آدَمَ خَلَقَهُ مِن تُرَابٍ ثُمَّ قَالَ لَهُ كُن فَيَكُونُ

*3:59 (Asad) Verily, in the sight of God, the nature of Jesus is as the nature of Adam, whom He created out of dust and then said unto him, "Be" - and he is.*

الْحَقُّ مِن رَّبِّكَ فَلاَ تَكُن مِّن الْمُمْتَرِينَ

*3:60 (Asad) [This is] the truth from thy Sustainer; be not, then, among the doubters!*

فَمَنْ حَآجَّكَ فِيهِ مِن بَعْدِ مَا جَاءكَ مِنَ الْعِلْمِ فَقُلْ تَعَالَوْاْ نَدْعُ أَبْنَاءنَا وَ أَبْنَاءكُمْ وَنِسَاءنَا وَنِسَاءكُمْ وَأَنفُسَنَا وَأَنفُسَكُمْ ثُمَّ نَبْتَهِلْ فَنَجْعَل لَّعْنَةُ اللّهِ عَلَى الْكَاذِبِينَ

*3:61 (Asad) And if anyone should argue with thee about this [truth] after all the knowledge that has come unto thee, say: "Come! Let us summon our sons and your sons, and our women and your women, and ourselves and yourselves; and then let us pray [together] humbly and ardently, and let us invoke God's curse upon those [of us] who are telling a lie."*

Muhammad recited the first two verses and, when the Christians refused to accept them, he recited the third verse (3:61) and challenged them to a Mubahala (imprecation: invoke the curse of Allah on the liars). The following day, the Christian priests came to confront Muhammad. Muhammad brought with him Hasan, Husayn, Fatimah, and Ali. When the Christians saw the confidence with which Muhammad had brought his infant grandsons, his daughter, and his son-in-law for imprecation (Mubahala). They backed out of the confrontation and agreed instead to a treaty to pay taxes.

According to Jabir Ibn Abdillah al-Ansari (a great companion of the Prophet), in verse 3:61 the word "sons" refers to al-Hasan and al-Husayn, the word "women" refers to Fatimah, and the word "our selves" refer to the Prophet and 'Ali'. [19]

At the time when the curse upon liars was being invoked, Muhammad could not have taken the risk of bringing anyone with a flawed background to Mubahala. Muhammad had to take only the five (Muhammad, Fatimah, Ali, Hasan and Husayn) highlighted by the Quran in "Aya Tatheer" who were pure and flawless. Quran mentions "Bring your women" and Muhammad had the option to take any or all his wives, but Muhammad only brought Fatimah. Quran mentioned "children", but he brought only his grandsons Hasan and Husayn. Similarly, the verse mentioned "anfusana" or "selves", but Muhammad did not go alone; he brought Ali with him. It is important to note here that Anfusana has a much greater and deeper meaning than the usual translation as "selves". (See note 1).

Muhammad Basically declared the purity and flawlessness of himself and these four individuals when it came to Mubahala. The possibility of the flawed past and future of some of his wives and others would have disqualified them from passing this test of integrity and honesty, and Muhammad could not have risked his prophethood (Nabuwat).

Sa'd Ibn Abi Waqqas [20] :

"...And when the verse 3:61 was revealed, the Prophet called 'Ali, Fatimah, al-Hasan, and al-Husayn. Then the Prophet said: 'O Lord! These are my family members (Ahli)'".

The overwhelming amount of information presented suggests that the wives were not included in the "Ahl al Bayt".

**Aya Muwaddah:**

"Aya Muwaddah" was revealed to address the believers, where Allah announced that the ideal way to receive rewards is to love Muhammad's kinfolk (al Quraba). The expression of love for Allah's chosen models (Ahl al Bayt) is intended to lead the believers on the right path or "sirat e mustaqeem".

$$ ذَلِكَ الَّذِي يُبَشِّرُ اللَّهُ عِبَادَهُ الَّذِينَ آمَنُوا وَعَمِلُوا الصَّالِحَاتِ قُل لَّا أَسْأَلُكُمْ عَلَيْهِ $$

$$ أَجْرًا إِلَّا الْمَوَدَّةَ فِي الْقُرْبَى وَمَن يَقْتَرِفْ حَسَنَةً نَّزِدْ لَهُ فِيهَا حُسْنًا إِنَّ اللَّهَ غَفُورٌ $$

$$ شَكُورٌ $$

*This it is which Allah announceth unto His bondmen who believe and do good works. Say (O Muhammad, unto mankind): I ask of you no fee therefor, save loving kindness among kinsfolk. And whoso scoreth a good deed we add unto its good for him. Lo! Allah is Forgiving, Responsive. 42:23 - (Picktall).*

Ibn Abbas narrated: "When the above verse was revealed, the companions asked: 'O' the Messenger of Allah! Who are those near kin whose love Allah has made obligatory for us?' Upon that the Prophet (S.A.W.) said: 'Ali, Fatimah, and their two sons.' He (S.A.W.) repeated this sentence thrice".[21]

An overwhelming number of Mufasereen and Muhaditheen have quoted that the word kinsfolk in *"I ask of you no fee therefor, save loving kindness towards **kinsfolk**"* is specifically referring to Fatimah, Ali, Hasan and Husayn. There are some who try to generalize and diminish the honor given by Muhammad to Fatimah and her family. Muhammad said that the **kinsfolk** or **kin** in this verse embodies Fatimah, Ali, Hasan and Husayn.

The following authors testify that the term "Ahl al Bayt" in the Quran represents Fatimah, Ali, Hasan, and Husayn. Of course, Muhammad is always the main element of "Ahl al Bayt":

Wilfred Madelung made the following observation on the verse referenced as the verse of purification [22]:

> *"Who are the 'people of the house' here? The pronoun referring to them is in the masculine plural, while the preceding part of the verse is in the feminine plural. This change of gender has evidently contributed to the birth of various accounts of a legendary character, attaching the latter part of the verse to the five People of the Mantle (ahl al-kisā'): Muhammad, 'Ali, Fātima, Hasan and Husayn. In spite of the obvious Shia significance, the great majority of the reports quoted by al-Tabari in his commentary on this verse support this interpretation."*

According to Laura Veccia Vaglieri in Encyclopaedia of Islam.[23]

*"A verse of the Ḳurʾān (XXXIII, 33) says: "God wishes only to remove from you the uncleanness, O People of the House" (Ahl al-bayt [q.v.]). The preceding verses contain instructions to the wives of the Prophet, and there the verbs and pronouns are in the feminine plural; but in this verse, addressed to the People of the House, the pronouns are in the masculine plural. Thus, it has been said, it is no longer a question of the Prophet's wives, or of them alone. To whom then does it refer? The expression Ahl al-bayt can only mean "Family of the Prophet". The privilege accorded by God to the latter (originally entirely spiritual, but later not merely so) naturally led all the relatives of Muḥammad—those nearest to him, those belonging to the collateral branches of the family, and beyond this such groups of the community as the Anṣār, or indeed the whole of the community—to claim a place in the Ahl al-bayt. But there is a story given in many traditions according to which Muḥammad sheltered under his cloak (or under a covering or under a sort of tent), in varying circumstances (including the occasion when he was preparing for the mubāhala), his grandchildren al-Ḥasan and al-Ḥusayn, his daughter Fāṭima and his son-in-law ʿAlī; and so it is these five who are given the title Ahl al-kisāʾ [q.v.] or "People of the Mantle". **Efforts have been made to include among the latter Muḥammad's wives; in general however the number of the privileged is limited to these five".***

**Ghadir e Khumm:**

The third and final event is "Ghadir e Khumm" (See Note 2). While ample evidence has been provided to illustrate the membership of the "Ahl al Bayt", for Ali, it is important to discuss the event known as "Ghadir e Khumm" to illustrate how Ali was essential to Muhammad and Islam. Ali had been honored with exceptional qualities that no one in the history of Islam had. He was born in Kaabah, was raised by Muhammad and was the first male to have openly pledged allegiance and support to Muhammad at the very first call to Islam known as "Da'wat dhu 'l-'Ashira" (See Note 3). Ali declared his commitment, repeatedly at the "Da'wat dhu 'l-'Ashira" to support Muhammad in every way he could to propagate Islam. Muhammad in response announced; "Verily this is my brother, my successor, and my caliph amongst you; therefore, listen to him and obey."

It is critically important at this stage to reflect upon the similarities between Muhammad and Ali. Unquestionably, these personalities complemented each other in the advancement of Islam. Saad Ibn Abu Waqas reports the following:

*"The Messenger of God took a journey to Tabook and he appointed 'Ali to succeed him in Medina. 'Ali said to the Prophet: 'Do you leave me with the children and the women?' The Messenger replied: 'Are you not satisfied to be to me like Aaron to Moses except that there shall be no Prophet after me'"?* [26]

The highlight of Muhammad's success in the completion of his assigned task depended on the delivery of one of the most important messages from Allah. This announcement about Ali's position, and his mission on the grounds of "Ghadir e Khumm", was so crucial that Allah had to strategically enshrine it between two verses of the Quran.

It is momentous that Allah made the acceptance of Muhammad's mission contingent upon the declaration of Ali's role after Muhammad. Allah ordered Muhammad with a warning that if he did not declare Ali his successor, it would obliterate all of the work he had done as the prophet of Islam.

يَا أَيُّهَا الرَّسُولُ بَلِّغْ مَا أُنزِلَ إِلَيْكَ مِن رَّبِّكَ وَإِن لَّمْ تَفْعَلْ فَمَا بَلَّغْتَ رِسَالَتَهُ وَاللّهُ يَعْصِمُكَ

مِنَ النَّاسِ إِنَّ اللّهَ لاَ يَهْدِي الْقَوْمَ الْكَافِرِينَ

*O Messenger! proclaim the (message) which hath been sent to thee from thy Lord. If thou didst not, thou wouldst not have fulfilled and proclaimed His mission. And Allah will defend thee from men (who mean mischief). For Allah guideth not those who reject Faith (5:67).*

Muhammad, among thousands (100,000 -125,000) of returning pilgrims from his last Hajj, stopped at a crucial juncture, built a stage, and delivered a lengthy sermon to the thousands, then lifted Ali's hands and said; *"Man kunto maula fa haza Ali un maula" (Whomever I am his master, this Ali is his master)* [27] and asked the attendees who had pledged their allegiance to him and to Islam, to also pledge their allegiance to Ali.[28] Among the thousands who pledged their allegiance to Ali were, notably, Abu Bakr, Umar, and Usman.[29]

This historic declaration was unique, and its aim was to consolidate and safeguard the future of Islam under the guardianship of Ali.

To summarize the events at Ghadir e Khumm:

The day at Ghadir e Khumm started by Allah ordering Muhammad:

يَا أَيُّهَا الرَّسُولُ بَلِّغْ مَا أُنزِلَ إِلَيْكَ مِن رَّبِّكَ وَإِن لَّمْ تَفْعَلْ فَمَا بَلَّغْتَ رِسَالَتَهُ وَاللّهُ

يَعْصِمُكَ مِنَ النَّاسِ إِنَّ اللّهَ لاَ يَهْدِي الْقَوْمَ الْكَافِرِينَ

*O Messenger! proclaim the (message) which hath been sent to thee from thy Lord. If thou didst not, thou wouldst not have fulfilled and proclaimed His mission. And Allah will defend thee from men (who mean mischief ). For Allah guideth not those who reject Faith (5:67).*

Muhammad responded by preparing the stage and declaring:

*"Man kunto maula fa haza Ali un maula". "Whomever I am his master, this Ali is his master".[27]*

Allah followed it by expressing his acceptance and completion of Muhammad's mission as follows:

الْيَوْمَ أَكْمَلْتُ لَكُمْ دِينَكُمْ وَأَتْمَمْتُ عَلَيْكُمْ نِعْمَتِي وَرَضِيتُ لَكُمُ الإِسْلاَمَ دِينًا

*This day have I perfected your religion for you, completed My favour upon you, and have chosen for you Islam as your religion (5:3).*

Muhammad culminated the day by asking the community to pledge their allegiance to Ali.

The event of "Ghadir e Khumm" itself is undeniably recognized on a bipartisan basis. The term Maula is therefore about a leader, a guardian, an administrator, and an authority on Islam and implementor of the Islamic laws (See Note 2).

The events of Mubahalah, Aya Muwaddah, and Ghadir e Khumm were presented to illustrate the identity of the "Ahl al Bayt" repeatedly declared my Muhammad.

In the beginning of the chapter, ahadith from the wives and the companions of Muhammad were presented. It is essential to provide one more testimony to resolve the dilemma about the "Ahl al Bayt" and the identity of the people of the "kisa" simply on the basis of the circumstances and the location of the revelation of "Aya Tatheer".

It is well known that this verse was delivered inside an enclosure, a specially created canopy (Kisa) by Muhammad where he gathered the selected five members to be classified as "Ahl al Bayt" under it as he prepared to receive the revelation of the "Aya Tatheer". Once the verse was delivered inside the "Kisa" canopy, it was impossible to include anyone besides the five. This strategically orchestrated setup eliminated all possibilities of including anyone who may have been present in that room but not under the "Kisa" canopy. Umm Salama and Aiysha recognized the importance of being part of the "Ahl al Bayt" and "Ahl al Kisa". They asked Muhammad for permission to enter it but were repeatedly denied.

Muhammad expressed love for these four personalities throughout his life. As discussed earlier, it was not Muhammad that was expressing his love; It was Allah's message that he was conveying to the mankind. Allah has said that Muhammad does not speak anything on his own accept what Allah instructs him to say (53:3,4). Examination of the lives of these four nearest members of his family indicates the key role they played in supporting Muhammad to propagate Islam. Allah, in return, endorsed their dedication to Islam from the events of the revelation of "Aya Tatheer", Mubahalah, Aya Muwaddah, and Ghadir e Khumm.

It is not surprising that these models of excellence surpassed all trials and tribulations with an unconditional submission to Allah. Every hadith and event presented reflects a small token of appreciation for their services.

A detailed analysis of all the seven verses will ensue in the next chapter to show how and why these verses are strategically constructed to deliver this critical message of leadership to the Islamic community "The Umma".

# Chapter 5

وَمَكَرُواْ وَمَكَرَ اللّهُ وَاللّهُ خَيْرُ الْمَاكِرِينَ

*And (the unbelievers) plotted and planned, and Allah too planned, and the best of planners is Allah. - 3:54* **(Y. Ali)**

### Gender Modulations in Verses 28 - 34

The gender modulations in these seven verses play a critical role in the characterization of what the term "Ahl al Bayt" represents. The pronouns have been color-coded for ease of the analyses of the gender format to enable characterization of the individuals being defined by the term "Ahl al Bayt". In addition, there are terms such as "Buyutekunna" and "ankum" that exhibit ancillary insight to the identity of the individuals that can conceivably makeup the term "Ahl al Bayt".

There are 27 words **highlighted in red** are Arabic terms that are all in the feminine plural pronoun form. The addressees are the wives of Muhammad and therefore the feminine plural gender is specifically used each time Muhammad's wives are being addressed. However, there are two Arabic terms highlighted in blue embedded in verse 33, "Aya Tatheer", which are in the masculine plural form, suggesting that the majority of addressees relating to the term "Ahl al Bayt" are males.

In addition, the Arabic term "Buyutekunna" highlighted in green refer to different homes in which Muhammad's wives lived in. This factor has a significant impact on the determination of whether the wives can be "ahl al Bayt".

*Al-Ahzab (The Confederates) - 33:28*

يَا أَيُّهَا النَّبِيُّ قُل لِّأَزْوَاجِكَ إِن كُنتُنَّ تُرِدْنَ الْحَيَاةَ الدُّنْيَا وَزِينَتَهَا فَتَعَالَيْنَ أُمَتِّعْكُنَّ

وَأُسَرِّحْكُنَّ سَرَاحًا جَمِيلًا

*Ya ayyuha alnnabiyyu qul liazwajika in kuntunna turidna alhayata alddunya wazeenataha fataAAalayna omattiAAkunna waosarrih kunna sarahan jameelan*

*O PROPHET! Say unto thy wives: "If you desire [but] the life of this world and its charms – well, then, I shall provide for you and release you in a becoming manner;(Asad).*

*Al-Ahzab (The Confederates) - 33:29*

وَإِن كُنتُنَّ تُرِدْنَ اللَّهَ وَرَسُولَهُ وَالدَّارَ الْآخِرَةَ فَإِنَّ اللَّهَ أَعَدَّ لِلْمُحْسِنَاتِ مِنكُنَّ أَجْرًا

عَظِيمًا

*Wain kuntunna turidna Allaha warasoolahu waalddara alakhirata fainna Allaha aAAadda lilmuhsinati minkunna ajran AAatheeman*

*but if you desire God and His Apostle, and [thus the good of] the life in the hereafter, then [know that], verily, for the doers of good among you God has readied a mighty reward!" (Asad)*

*Al-Ahzab (The Confederates) - 33:30*

يَا نِسَاء النَّبِيِّ مَن يَأْتِ مِنكُنَّ بِفَاحِشَةٍ مُّبَيِّنَةٍ يُضَاعَفْ لَهَا الْعَذَابُ ضِعْفَيْنِ وَكَانَ

ذَلِكَ عَلَى اللَّهِ يَسِيرًا

*Ya nisaa alnnabiyyi* man yati *minkunna* bifa<u>h</u>ishatin mubayyinatin yuda<u>AA</u>af *laha* al<u>AA</u>a<u>th</u>abu <u>d</u>i<u>AA</u>fayni wak<u>a</u>na <u>tha</u>lika <u>AA</u>al<u>a</u> All<u>a</u>hi yaseera**n**

*O wives of the Prophet! If any of you were to become guilty of manifestly immoral conduct, double [that of other sinners] would be her suffering [in the hereafter]: for that is indeed easy for God. (Asad)*

*Al-Ahzab (The Confederates) – 33:31*

وَمَن يَقْنُتْ مِنكُنَّ لِلَّهِ وَرَسُولِهِ وَتَعْمَلْ صَالِحًا نُّؤْتِهَا أَجْرَهَا مَرَّتَيْنِ وَأَعْتَدْنَا لَهَا

رِزْقًا كَرِيمًا

*Waman yaqnut minkunna lill<u>a</u>hi waras<u>oo</u>lihi wata<u>AA</u>mal <u>sa</u>li<u>h</u>an nutih<u>a</u> ajra ha marratayni wa<u>aAA</u>tadn<u>a</u> lah<u>a</u> rizqan kareem**an***

*But if any of you devoutly obeys God and His Apostle and does good deeds, on her shall We bestow her reward twice-over: for We shall have readied for her a most excellent sustenance [in the life to come].Al-Ahzab (The Confederates) – 33:31 (Asad)*

*Al-Ahzab (The Confederates) – 33:32*

يَا نِسَاء النَّبِيِّ لَسْتُنَّ كَأَحَدٍ مِّنَ النِّسَاء إِنِ اتَّقَيْتُنَّ فَلَا تَخْضَعْنَ بِالْقَوْلِ فَيَطْمَعَ الَّذِي فِي قَلْبِهِ مَرَضٌ وَقُلْنَ قَوْلًا مَّعْرُوفًا

*Ya nisaa alnnabiyyi lastunna kaahadin mina alnnisai ini ittaqaytunna fala takhdaAAna bialqawli fayatmaAAa allathee fee qalbihi maradun waqulna qawlan maAAroofan*

*O wives of the Prophet! You are not like any of the [other] women, provided that you remain [truly] conscious of God. Hence, be not over-soft in your speech, lest any whose heart is diseased should be moved to desire [you]: but, withal, speak in a kindly way. (Asad)*

*Al-Ahzab (The Confederates) - 33:33*

وَقَرْنَ فِي بُيُوتِكُنَّ وَلَا تَبَرَّجْنَ تَبَرُّجَ الْجَاهِلِيَّةِ الْأُولَى وَأَقِمْنَ الصَّلَاةَ وَآتِينَ الزَّكَاةَ وَأَطِعْنَ اللَّهَ وَرَسُولَهُ إِنَّمَا يُرِيدُ اللَّهُ لِيُذْهِبَ عَنكُمُ الرِّجْسَ أَهْلَ الْبَيْتِ وَيُطَهِّرَكُمْ تَطْهِيرًا

*Waqarna fee buyootikunna wala tabarrajna tabarruja aljahiliyyati aloola waaqimna alssalata waateena alzzakata waatiAAna Allaha warasoolahu innama yureedu Allahu liyuthhiba AAankumu alrrijsa ahla albayti wayutahhirakum tatheeran*

*And abide quietly in your homes, and do not flaunt your charms as they used to flaunt them in the old days of pagan ignorance; and be constant in prayer, and render the purifying dues, and pay heed unto God and His Apostle: for God only wants to remove from you all that might be loathsome, O you members of the [Prophet's] household, and to purify you to utmost purity. (Asad)*

*Al-Ahzab (The Confederates) - 33:34*

وَاذْكُرْنَ مَا يُتْلَى فِي بُيُوتِكُنَّ مِنْ آيَاتِ اللَّهِ وَالْحِكْمَةِ إِنَّ اللَّهَ كَانَ لَطِيفًا خَبِيرًا

*Waothkurna ma yutla fee buyootikunna min ayati Allahi waalhikmati inna Allaha kana lateefan khabeeran*

*And bear in mind all that is recited in your homes of God's messages and [His] wisdom: for God is unfathomable [in His wisdom], all-aware. (Asad)*

These above seven verses are all about the wives of Muhammad except for a strategically embedded segment within them to introduce a group of individuals created by Allah with extraordinary attributes of purity in "Aya Tatheer". Gender modulations are the focus of this chapter. It is very interesting to note that in all these seven verses, a female gender is used except in "Aya Tatheer" where a dramatic shift to male plural gender takes place. Why would this shift take place?

An extremely important point to note is that the term "Ahl al Bayt" has never been used anywhere in these verses where Muhammad's wives are being addressed.

Verse 33 begins by addressing the wives of Muhammad in the feminine plural form. With the part beginning with "*Innama youriallah…*", the gender suddenly switches from feminine plural to masculine plural gender "*ankum*" and "*yutahhirakum*", highlighted in blue indicating that the addressees are no longer the wives of Muhammad but rather a majority male group where one or more woman can be included.

It is not just the modulation in the gender but a change in tone that insinuates a separate group of individuals who are viewed as "pure" by Allah. Prior to this verse, where the wives of Muhammad are being addressed, it is in strict terms of punishments, moral and ethical restrictions, castigating coquettish or provocative behavior, and warnings against general misbehavior. The language and tone suddenly transition from cautioning and punitive to loving and protective format when The Quran speaks of the "Ahl al Bayt". This dramatic change in tone defines the difference between the wives of Muhammad and his "Ahl al Bayt" in this verse.

In addition to gender modulation, the word "Buyutekunna" in verses 33 and 34 highlighted in green adds a distinctive and unequivocal solution to the dilemma of how the word "Bayt" is characterized in the term "Ahl al Bayt". Verse 33 starts with "Buyutekunna", which is translated as **houses** or **households**, and is a feminine plural possessive pronoun first used in verse 33:33 right before "Aya Tatheer", referring to the several houses in which Muhammad's wives lived. Verse 33 starts with "Buyutekunna" referring to the several **houses** in which the wives lived but then switches to "al Bayt" in "Aya Tatheer" which refers to **a single household**. "Buyutekunna" has been used twice in this set of seven verses addressing the wives. First, in verse 33 and second time in verse 34, both times addressing his wives in connection to their houses. The term "Buyutekunna" is specifically used to address the wives of Muhammad living in different homes and is one of the most important factors that disqualifies them from being part of single particular household referred to as "Ahl al Bayt".

Hypothetically speaking if this verse was about the wives, it ("Aya Tatheer") would have been revealed in all feminine plural form as in the previous verses to read, *"Innama Yuridallah hu Liyuzhiba ankunna* <u>rigsa ya nisa an nabi</u> *wa yutahhirakunna tatheera"* (Allah's intention is to keep away all abominations from you "<u>o' wives of the prophet</u>" and keep <u>you all</u> pure and spotless) **or** *"Innama Yuridallah hu Liyuzhiba ankunna* <u>rigsa ahl buyutekunna</u> *wa yutahhirakunna tatheera"* (Allah's intention is to keep away all abominations from you "people of households" and keep you all pure and spotless) . The terms *Ankum* would have changed to *Ankunna,* "Ahl al Bayt" would have been replaced by *"Ya nisa an nabi"* or *"Ya azwajun Nabih"* (oh wives of the prophet as in verses 28-33) and *yutathhirakum* to *yutathhirakunna,* to convert the entire "Aya Tatheer" into all feminine plural form.

وَتَمَّتْ كَلِمَتُ رَبِّكَ صِدْقًا وَ عَدْلاً لاَّ مُبَدِّلِ لِكَلِمَاتِهِ وَهُوَ السَّمِيعُ الْعَلِيمُ

*The word of your Lord is complete, in truth and justice. <u>Nothing shall abrogate His words.</u> He is the Hearer, the Omniscient. [Quran 6:115]*

However, the final words of Allah in Quran are: *Innama Yuridallah hu Liyuzhiba <u>ankum</u> al rigsa <u>Ahl al Bayt</u> wa <u>yutahhirakum</u> tatheera.* The Quran clearly transitions here to masculine plural, meaning this can only be about a mostly male group.

As has already been discussed, Muhammad has repeatedly declared who his "Ahl al Bayt" are. Muhammad, Fatimah, Ali, Hassan, and Husayn, the group he declared as his "Ahl al Bayt", are mostly male and the masculine plural gender works to further cement whom exactly "Aya Tatheer" is referring to.

Chapter 6 unfolds the setup of every word of "Aya Tatheer" that this book is about.

The next chapter addresses some of the most crucial aspects of "Aya Tatheer". The grammatical unfolding of every word of "Aya Tatheer" demonstrates who possibly can be part of the term "Ahl al Bayt".

ذَلِكَ الْكِتَابُ لاَ رَيْبَ فِيهِ هُدًى لِّلْمُتَّقِينَ

*This is the Scripture whereof there is no doubt, a guidance unto those who ward off (evil). – 2:2 (Picktall)*

الَر كِتَابٌ أُحْكِمَتْ آيَاتُهُ ثُمَّ فُصِّلَتْ مِن لَّدُنْ حَكِيمٍ خَبِيرٍ

*A Book whose verses have been perfected. 11:1*

وَتَمَّتْ كَلِمَتُ رَبِّكَ صِدْقًا وَعَدْلاً لاَّ مُبَدِّلِ لِكَلِمَاتِهِ وَهُوَ السَّمِيعُ الْعَلِيمُ

*The word of your Lord is complete, in truth and justice. Nothing shall abrogate His words. He is the Hearer, the Omniscient. [Quran 6:115]*

## "Aya Tatheer" - Syntax and Grammar

Quran, Islam and Muhammad are inseparable. The equilibrium between chapters, verses, and words is exquisite. Every word of Quran is delicately crafted to convey a specific message for a balanced life. Quran, as it claims, is absolute and perfect and all doors for modification or alteration are sealed. The central theme of this book is "Haqq" and "Ahl al Bayt". The following three verses are about "Haqq" or "truth", and justice:

شَهْرُ رَمَضَانَ الَّذِيَ أُنزِلَ فِيهِ الْقُرْآنُ هُدًى لِّلنَّاسِ وَبَيِّنَاتٍ مِّنَ الْهُدَى وَ الْفُرْقَانِ

فَمَن شَهِدَ مِنكُمُ الشَّهْرَ فَلْيَصُمْهُ وَمَن كَانَ مَرِيضًا أَوْ عَلَى سَفَرٍ فَعِدَّةٌ مِّنْ أَيَّامٍ

أُخَرَ يُرِيدُ اللّهُ بِكُمُ الْيُسْرَ وَ لاَ يُرِيدُ بِكُمُ الْعُسْرَ وَلِتُكْمِلُواْ الْعِدَّةَ وَلِتُكَبِّرُواْ اللّهَ عَلَى

مَا هَدَاكُمْ وَلَعَلَّكُمْ تَشْكُرُونَ

*It was the month of Ramadan in which the Qur'an was [first] bestowed from on high as a guidance unto man and a self-evident proof of that guidance, and as the standard by which to discern the true from the false. 2:185 (Asad)*

إِنَّ هَـذَا الْقُرْآنَ يِهْدِي لِلَّتِي هِيَ أَقْوَمُ وَيُبَشِّرُ الْمُؤْمِنِينَ الَّذِينَ يَعْمَلُونَ

الصَّالِحَاتِ أَنَّ لَهُمْ أَجْرًا كَبِيرًا

*"Lo! this Quran guideth unto that which is straightest, and giveth tidings unto the believers who do good works that theirs will be a great reward." 17:9 (Picktall)*

الَر كِتَابٌ أَنزَلْنَاهُ إِلَيْكَ لِتُخْرِجَ النَّاسَ مِنَ الظُّلُمَاتِ إِلَى النُّورِ بِإِذْنِ رَبِّهِمْ

إِلَى صِرَاطِ الْعَزِيزِ الْحَمِيدِ

*"A Book We have sent down to you so that you may bring forth mankind from the darkness into the light......". (14:1)*

Likewise, every word of every verse in these seven verses (28-34) surrounding the "Aya Tatheer" are impeccably balanced. It is "Haqq" that shines from every verse setup in this sequence of verses. Love, advice, and warnings are all presented in a unique way with deep undertones to serve a purpose. Allah has taken exceptional care in selecting the precise words and terms to characterize a chosen group of individuals whom he defines as "pure" in this verse.

It is critical at this point to analyze every word of "Aya Tatheer" on a grammatical basis to understand the extraordinary moral and ethical values delivered in this verse.

"Aya Tatheer":

> *Innama Yurid Allah ho Liyuzhiba ankum alrigsa Ahl al Bayt wayutahhirakum tatheera*

> Ideally it would be demonstrated that the accurate translation of this part of the verse must be:

> *"It is Allah's intention to keep away all abominations from **only you** "Ahl al Bayt" and to keep you thoroughly pure".*

There are roughly 16 words in "Aya Tatheer", depending on the syntax of how these words are coupled.

The syntax and semantics of "Aya Tatheer" play a key role in the unique makeup of the sentence, pinpointing at the essential components of the term "Ahl al Bayt". There are several terms and words of "Aya Tatheer" that have had a manufactured controversy applied to them, as some attempt to apply their own religious biases to adjust its meaning. As discussed earlier with examples like Maududi, many exegetes attempt to play interpretative verbal gymnastics to include anyone they believe should be within this verse.

Here, the syntax of this verse will be analyzed to see all possible interpretations and conclude on what the most logical translation of these terms would be.

<u>*"Innama"*:</u>

The first word *"Innama"* is usually translated as "verily". This translation is imprecise as applied to this verse. *"Innama"* is made up of *"inna"* and *"ma"*, imposing an exclusivity with boundaries attached to it. *"Innama"* can be interpreted in different ways; here, it takes the meaning of "none other than this", "only", "indeed" and "just this and nothing else". *Innama* is *Kalima e hasr* which means it has a target and is directed on a specific object. Whether the object is "Ahl al Bayt" or not will become clear with further analysis. The following four verses of Quran starting with the term *Innama* are discussed to elucidate the intended purpose of its use in "Aya Tatheer".

Surah Maidah verse 55:

إِنَّمَا وَلِيُّكُمُ اللّٰهُ وَرَسُولُهُ وَالَّذِينَ آمَنُواْ الَّذِينَ يُقِيمُونَ الصَّلَاةَ وَيُؤْتُونَ

الزَّكَاةَ وَهُمْ رَاكِعُونَ

*Innama Waliyu kum allah wa rasoolahu wallazina amanul lazina yoqemunas salata wa you tunas zakata wa hum raki oon.*

*No one except Allah is your Wali (master) and His Messenger and those who believe, those who keep up prayers and pay the poor-rate **while** they bow.*

*Innama* in this case would be translated as "only Allah, Muhammad and the one who gave "Zakaat" (gave alms to the needy) during the posture of *ruku* are (is) *Wali* (*ruku* is the position of bowing one's head in prayer, and *rakioon* is the action of bowing one's head in prayer). The context in which the word *Wali* is used in this verse is about a guardian/master. (See note 1).

There are significant differences of opinion between the exegetes in the translation of the last part of the verse starting from "*wallazina amanul lazina yoqemunas salata wa you tunas zakata wa hum raki oon.*" It is usually translated as "those that are constant in prayer, render the purifying dues, and bow down". This translation is misleading and does not agree with the well documented event in history where Ali gave the poor alms while bowing down in his prayer. This is discussed in detail in note 1 (See Note 1). When Muhammad was informed of Ali giving away his ring as "*zakat*" (alms) during his prayer, it was at that moment that Allah revealed this verse declaring Ali as *Wali* in the same context with Muhammad. Therefore, an accurate translation would be: "*those who keep up prayers, pay the poor **while** they bow*". "*Wa hum*" translated to "*While*" appears to be more logical because it is about a process represented by the word "*rakioon*", which describes a process in a present continuous tense of giving "*zakat*" while in the act of "*ruku*"*(to bow down in prostration)*. Scholars have discussed in detail about why it should be translated as "*pay the poor **while** they bow*". This is like the term "*yuqimoonas salat*" (observe regular prayers) which expresses executing regular prayers as an ongoing act.

The deliverance of this verse specifically after Ali had given away his ring during his prayer is a testification of Allah's acceptance of this gesture of Ali and consequentially, publicly lifting him to the status of *Wilayat* in this verse. (See note 1 on *Wilayat*)

Interestingly, the most important point to note is that the term "*Innama*" in this verse can best be interpreted as: Only Allah is the *Wali* (master), and Muhammad is also a *Wali* (under the authority of Allah), "and those (meaning Ali) who keep up prayers, pay the poor **while** they bow" is (are)*Wali*.

Surah Ya Sin verse 82 : is the second verse that starts with *Innama* :

$$إِنَّمَا أَمْرُهُ إِذَا أَرَادَ شَيْئًا أَنْ يَقُولَ لَهُ كُنْ فَيَكُونُ$$

*"Innama amruhu itha iarada shayan an yaqoola lahu kun fayakoon".*

*His Being alone is such that when He wills a thing to be, He but says unto it, "Be" — and it is. - 36:82 (Asad) -*

The word *Innama* in this verse, when examined in the context of the preceding and succeeding verses, brings out the true meaning that Allah alone has the power to create anything instantaneously.

The term *Amruhu* is a command, while the term *irada* is the intention. The connection between these terms is uniquely associated only with Allah. Allah's intention becomes his command to create; he says "to be", and thus, it is created. Implied by this verse is Allah's ability to create anything at any time instantly, which further exemplifies his "oneness", as he "alone" can do so.

Surah Ta-HA verse 98: is the third verse starting with *Innama* :

إِنَّمَا إِلَهُكُمُ اللَّهُ الَّذِي لَا إِلَهَ إِلَّا هُوَ وَسِعَ كُلَّ شَيْءٍ عِلْمًا

*Innama ilahukumu Allahu allathee la ilaha illa huwa wasiAAa kulla shayin AAilman*

*Your only deity is God - He save whom there is no deity, [and whho] embraces all things within His knowledge!" 20:98 (Asad)*

Surah Al -Anbiya verse 108: Is the fourth verse with *Innama*:

قُلْ إِنَّمَا يُوحَى إِلَيَّ أَنَّمَا إِلَهُكُمْ إِلَهٌ وَاحِدٌ فَهَلْ أَنتُم مُّسْلِمُونَ

*fQul innama yooha ilayya annama ilahukum ilahun wahidun fahal antum muslimoona*

*Say: "It has but been revealed unto me that your God is the One and Only God: will you, then, surrender yourselves unto Him?" 21:108 (Asad)*

In all, the verses presented starting with *Innama* meaning "only" describe the exclusivity of this term with Allah in defining his "Oneness", pronouncing the concept of Tawheed. *Innama* is used to illustrate the myriad attributes of Allah to further define "Tawheed".

Similarly these verses present the uniqueness of the term *Innama* in *"Aya Tatheer"* that targets the object "Ahl al Bayt" relating to the creation of **only** a small group of individuals established by the term "Ahl al Bayt".

### *"Yourid Allahhu":*

The second term, *Yourid Allahhu*, is generally translated as "Allah wants to"; This is, in fact, far from what it is intended to mean. Further analysis will show that *Yurid Allahhu* takes a different translation when combined with *Innama*. The best translation of these terms together would be, "it is none other than Allah's intention". Allah's *irada* or intention is defined by Quran from the statement *"kun fa ya koon"* (be and it is) Surah Yasin verse 82, which was discussed earlier. Allah is declaring his intention at the beginning of the sentence by the term *Yourid Allahhu* to keep away all abominations from "Ahl al Bayt". It is important to note that "Ahl al Bayt" is a masculine plural object. This term falls under the classification of *"iradatel takwiniya"*, which defines the "will" or intention" of the Almighty Allah that transforms simultaneously into action to complete its intended objective. Allah's "will" is not bound by time, and thus, there is no time lapse between Allah's "will" to create and its creation. Anything that Allah intends, or "wills" is guaranteed to happen permanently. *"Iradatul takwiniya"* is therefore generative and is guaranteed to take immediate effect.

On the contrary, the *"Iradatul tashriya"* is a legislative "will" and is dependent on an action taken by an individual who is required and advised to perform a task that he fulfils which lasts on a temporary basis. A typical example is the required ablution by a believer cleansing his/her hands and feet in preparation for prayer which is on a temporary basis and generally must be repeated if the cleanliness is not maintained for the upcoming prayer. Since, in "Aya Tatheer", it is Allah's intention (*Yourid Allahhu*) to "keep away all abominations from "Ahl al Bayt", this falls in the category of *"Tiradatul takwiniya"* which is guaranteed to be executed.

### *Liyuzhiba:*

The third word *Liyuzhiba*, defined as "to remove", is an elusive paraphrasing of the term. *Liyuzhiba* is a 3rd person masculine imperfect verb. The context in which the term *Liyuzhiba* is mentioned in "Aya Tatheer" implies "to keep away" all abominations (*rigs*) exclusively from "Ahl al Bayt". Unfortunately, scholars have interpreted *Liyuzhiba* to mean "to remove" instead of "to keep away" suggesting that "Ahl al Bayt" had *rigs* that was removed. Since the terminology of this term is controversial, it is important to take a moment and analyze the issue. The term *Liyuzhiba* or "to keep away" is connected to *Yuridallahhu*, or the intention of Allah, therefore is not bound by time. Grammatically, the accurate translation would be "to keep away" which will become apparent while discussing the word *Ankum* in the next section.

### *Ankum:*

The fourth word *Ankum* is translated as "you", referring to "Ahl al Bayt". *Ankum* is a **masculine plural** object addressing males with possible inclusion of one or more females. The *Ankum* masculine pronoun is significant because its object is the term "Ahl al Bayt" and the noun *Al Rigsa*. The combination of the terms *Liyuzhiba Ankum* would therefore be translated to *"to keep you away"* or *"to protect you"* or *"to prevent you"*. The term *Liyuzhiba* has deep connotations. The common mistake by translators is to translate *Liyuzhiba* as "to remove".

If *Liyuzhiba* was juxtaposed to *minkum* which is "from you", then *Liyuzhiba Minkum* would appropriately be translated "to remove from you". Since Quran explicitly uses *Liyuzhiba Ankum* and not *Liyuzhiba Minkum*, the only possible translation of *Liyuzhiba ankum* would be "to keep you away" or "to protect you". The target object is *Ankum* or "you" meaning "Ahl al Bayt". These terms *Liyuzhiba ankum*, and "Ahl al Bayt" can be translated properly in context of the terms *al rigsa*, which will be examined in the next section sub-titled *al rigsa*.

Another essential aspect associated with the term *Ankum* is with respect to the gender modulation. One would be able to determine on the gender basis if the wives of Muhammad are a part of "Ahl al Bayt". If wives were "Ahl al Bayt", *Ankum* in this verse would have been replaced by *Ankunna*, a feminine plural gender repeatedly used in previous verses addressing the wives. *Ankunna* was used in verses 29,30 and 31 addressing the wives and not in the "Aya Tatheer" (discussed in chapter 5).

## *Al Rigsa:*

The fifth word is, *al Rigsa* usually translated as "uncleanliness", "Abomination", "filthiness", "dirt", etcetera, and includes all forms of spiritual and physical uncleanliness. "Al" placed before *Rigsa* makes it all inclusive or all types of *Rigsa*. Hence it represents protection from any or all kinds of uncleanliness. This is an essential characteristic leading to the guaranteed purity of the group of individuals representing "Ahl al Bayt". This is huge because this is the only place in Quran where Allah himself has taken the responsibility of keeping away "all" and "any" type of impurity from "Ahl al bayt". Basically, this is the ultimate purity of divinely selected individuals identified as models of excellence termed as "Ahl al Bayt".

Ideally, the translation thus far of "Aya Tatheer" would be:

*"It is Allah's intention to keep away all abominations from **only you** "Ahl al Bayt".*

*Or*

*"It is Allah's intention to keep away all abominations from **none other than you** "Ahl al Bayt".*

*Ahl al Bayt:*

The sixth word, "Ahl al Bayt" has become the most controversial term. Translated as "members of the [Prophet's] household" or "people of the house", these words have been generalized to subvert prophet Muhammad's and the Quran's intended scope. The term "Ahl al Bayt" must be linguistically separated into its constitutional parts to identify all the essential components. Contemplating words and their associations particularly in the complex term "Ahl al Bayt" needs careful investigations both through powerful logical reasoning and grammatical clarifications.

The term "Ahl al Bayt" is essentially made up of three components:

- "Ahl",

- "al",

- "Bayt".

"Ahl": is family or people,

"al": is "this", and

"Bayt": is "home or household".

Therefore, "Ahl al Bayt" would be accurately translated as "people of **this** house" or "people of **this** household". The syllable "al" plays a vital role because it pinpoints to a specific place, time, thing or action. An example is a part of verse 3 of surah Maidah:

الْيَوْمَ أَكْمَلْتُ لَكُمْ دِينَكُمْ وَأَتْمَمْتُ عَلَيْكُمْ نِعْمَتِي وَرَضِيتُ لَكُمُ الإِسْلاَمَ دِينًا

*This (al) day* *have I perfected your religion for you, completed My favor upon you,*
*and have chosen for you Islam as your religion. But if any is forced by hunger, with no*
*inclination to transgression, Allah is indeed Oft-forgiving, Most Merciful. (Y.Ali)*
*(part of 5:3)*

A second translation of same verse is:

*Today* *have I perfected your religious law for you, and have bestowed upon you the full*
*measure of My blessings, and willed that self-surrender unto Me shall be your religion.*
*(Part of 5:3).*

A portion of the above verse from surah Maidah starts with *Al Youm* translated either as "**This day**"
or "**today**". "Al" (this) in this verse specifies a particular day of importance which is not like any other day.
Likewise, "al" is setup in "al Bayt" in the same way as "al" is set up in *al youm*, except that in the case of "al
Bayt", Allah is declaring the specificity of a particular household or an exclusive household of Muhammad.
The significance of the syllable "al" preceding "Bayt" emphasizes the fact that "Ahl al Bayt" is about the
"people of **this** (single) selected household". Since "Ahl al Bayt" is about the people of a particular household
of Muhammad, it is not possible that the term "Ahl al Bayt" can be about prophet Muhammad's wives as
they all lived in different homes.

Quran specifically addresses Muhammad's wives in the context of their homes in the beginning of
verse 33 by the term *Buyutekunna* which is plural for households.

Quran has used *Buyutekunna* in verse 33 and 34 distinctively to address several households in which
Muhammad's wives lived. The difference between the application of the terms "Ahl al Bayt" and *Buyutekunna*
in these verses is significant because in one case it is about a **single specific household** (Ahl al Bayt),
and in the other case it is about several households (*Buyutekunna*) because Muhammad's wives resided in
different homes.

Hence, the term "Ahl al Bayt" in verse 33:33 is only about the people of a selected household of Muhammad declared by him which included Fatimah, Ali, Hasan and Husayn.

*Wa Yutahhirakum Tatheera:*

*Wa* is translated as "and" is a conjunctive and "*Yutahhirakum*" – "to keep you pure" is a 3ʳᵈ person masculine, while *kum* makes it a masculine plural pronoun. *Wayutahhirakum* would be translated as "and to keep you pure" making this term masculine plural.

The last word *Tatheera* is a masculine noun generally translated as "with thorough purification". The issue with translations is that they do not accurately deliver the meaning and the associated message it is supposed to convey. *Wayutahhirakum Tatheera* would be translated as "and to keep you pure with thorough purification". These are "Ahl al Bayt" that Allah is taking the responsibility of creating them pure and flawless.

Notice that Allah in the following verse 125 of Surah Baqarah is ordering Abraham and Ismail to sanctify a particular house which Allah calls "My House":

وَإِذْ جَعَلْنَا الْبَيْتَ مَثَابَةً لِّلنَّاسِ وَأَمْناً وَاتَّخِذُواْ مِن مَّقَامِ إِبْرَاهِيمَ مُصَلًّى وَعَهِدْنَا

إِلَى إِبْرَاهِيمَ وَإِسْمَاعِيلَ أَن طَهِّرَا بَيْتِيَ لِلطَّائِفِينَ وَالْعَاكِفِينَ وَالرُّكَّعِ السُّجُودِ

*Remember We made the House a place of assembly for men and a place of safety; and take ye the station of Abraham as a place of prayer; and We covenanted with Abraham and Isma'il, that they should sanctify My House for those who compass it round, or use it as a retreat, or bow, or prostrate themselves (therein in prayer). - 2:125 (Y. Ali)*

Allah is directing Abraham and Isma'il to clean and purify "tahhira baytiya" by claiming Kaabah as "My House". Basically, Allah is referring to "Kaabah" as a particular house which he calls **His** house. This is similar to "al Bayt", a singular special household. In this case Allah is ordering Abraham and Ismail to keep **His** house pure, whereas in "Aya Tatheer" Allah **Himself** is taking the responsibility of creating the "Ahl al Bayt" pure.

The term *Yutahhirakum Tatheera* cannot be expressed in words unless an unorthodox methodology is applied to magnify its depth and breadth; to uncover its hidden treasures. The terms *Liyuzhiba* and *Yutahhirakum Tatheera* has special attributes attached to them. These essential aspects were not discussed in previous chapters. These attributes are addressed in greater detail in the next chapter.

# Chapter 7

كِتَابٌ أُحْكِمَتْ آيَاتُهُ ثُمَّ فُصِّلَتْ مِن لَّدُنْ حَكِيمٍ خَبِيرٍ

*(This is) a Scripture the revelations whereof are perfected and then expounded.*

*(It cometh) from One Wise, Informed, - 11:1* **(Picktall)**

## "Liyuzhiba" and "Yutahhirakum tatheera"

The terms *"Liyuzhiba"* and *"Yuthaherakum Tatheera"* have been discussed briefly in the previous chapters, however there are unique attributes about these terms that were purposely left out for in depth exploration.

The symbiotic relationship between the terms *Liyuzhiba* and *Yutahhirakum Tatheera* is significant and must be discussed to appreciate its connection to the term "Ahl al Bayt".

In the term *"Yuthahhirakum Tatheera"*, the "purity" declared here is the apex of the concept of pureness and spotlessness, as it is Allah the Creator who has taken responsibility for their purity. As discussed, attempts had been made to translate *"yutahhirakum tatheera"* as "purify you with thorough purification". This translation is inaccurate and does not justify the sheer complexity and excellence attached to this term, where their purity is being established on a divine scale of impeccability. Thus, *"Yutahhirakum Tatheera"*, at best can be translated as **"keep you pure at the divine scale of purity"**.

To fully appreciate the interdependence of the terms *"Liyzhiba"* and *"Yutahhirakum Tatheera"* it would be necessary to sequentially evaluate these terms.

*Liyuzhiba*:

The term *Liyuzhiba* has been used only once in the Quran. The context in which it is used defines its intended purpose. As previously discussed, it is inaccurately translated as; "to remove" which does not represent the continuity of purity that Allah had assigned only to "Ahl al Bayt". "To remove" implies that a condition existed and was removed. In the case of the "Ahl al Bayt", that is Muhammad, Ali, Fatimah, Hasan and Husayn, this translation "to remove" *Rigs* (abominations) would be, according to Islamic doctrine, flawed because Hasan and Husayn, who were about 6 and 5 years old at the time of the revelation of this verse, would be classified as Masoom. This is because all children of this age are, technically speaking, from the Islamic jurisprudential point of view, are Masoom (an innocent, one who cannot commit a sin, has no tendency towards sins and Allah keeps him/her away from sins and are therefore considered pure). Therefore "to remove" abominations that never existed in the case of a Masoom (Hasan and Husayn) would be incorrect.

In addition, Muhammad was created as Masoom. Allah in Quran has repeatedly said that Muhammad was free from flaws (see Note 1). Since Allah has created his prophet with the quality of inerrancy, therefore "to remove" something that never existed in Muhammad would be irresponsible. At least three members out of five would be classified as free from *rigs*. The term *Liyuzhiba* as stated in the Quran applies to all the members that makeup "Ahl al Bayt", thus this quality must include all. If one out of this group was classified as pure, the others will automatically be considered pure. Hence, the only translation that would accurately represent *Liyuzhiba* would be along the lines of "to keep away" suggesting that *rigs* or abominations never existed in the case of "Ahl al Bayt".

The second term *Yutahhirakum Tatheera* discussed in the next section complements the term *Liyuzhiba* and bolsters the purity of "Ahl al Bayt".

*Yutahhirakum Tatheera*:

This term is generally translated as "to purify you to utmost purity", "to purify you completely", "cleanse you with a thorough cleansing", "to purify you with [extensive] purification", "purify you (with) a thorough purification", and "to keep you pure and spotless". These mistranslations are varied attempts by exegetes (mufasereen) to weaken what these terms represent and dilute the magnitude of the purity emphasized here.

The selection of these words by Allah is to make this phrase unique. The term *Yutahhirakum Tatheera* has been used only once in the entire Quran and that too, only to characterize the "Ahl al Bayt".

There are two parts, *"Yutahhirakum"* and *"Tatheera"*, that complement each other. The purity of "Ahl al Bayt" defined by *"Yutahhirakum"* was reemphasized and redefined by the term *"Tatheera"*. It is Allah the creator who is declaring in the Quran in the following verse that it is in **HIS** infinite power to create, and **HE** has coined the term *"Yutahhirakum Tatheera"*.

> *And they returned with Grace and bounty from Allah. no harm ever touched them: For they followed the good pleasure of Allah. And Allah is the Lord of bounties unbounded. -3:174* **(Y. Ali)**

> • *He selecteth for HIS mercy whom He will. ALLAH IS of infinite bounty. - 3:74 (Picktall)*

The purity delineated in this part of the verse is beyond human intellectual capacity, because it is none other than Allah who has taken the responsibility for the purity of "Ahl al Bayt". Hence, to define purity attributed to "Ahl al Bayt" by Allah would require us to cross all the lines of our imagination and still fail to understand the level of purity implied. On human scale, *"Yutahhirakum Tatheera"*, at best can be translated as **"keep you (Ahl al Bayt) pure at the divine scale of purity"**.

# Chapter 8

وَمَا آتَاكُمُ الرَّسُولُ فَخُذُوهُ

*And whatsoever the messenger giveth you, take it. 59:7* **(Picktall)**

## Summary and Conclusions

The truth can be difficult. It can lie before our eyes and remain shielded, and some truths struggle to break free. For 1400 years, "Aya Tatheer" has survived countless redefinitions, interpretations, and biases. It has remained quiet but vigilant, ever ready to leap forward in a blast of consciousness, awakened before the eyes of those ready to go deep in the nuances, the sheer complexity and beauty that it extrapolates and imbibes within those select few, the "Ahl al Bayt".

Many have tried to subdue it, to dilute it, but none have been able to remove its magnetic power. There is something to be said about controversies and a myriad of interpretations clamoring to change "Aya Tatheer's" meanings; This verse **must** be of tremendous importance if they're all desperately fighting to make it stand for what they want it to mean.

And yet, no matter how hard they try, that shining light of truth, that unmistakable reality, mined from "Aya Tatheer's" words through intense deliberation, fact finding, and most importantly, listening to what these words say and not what **we** want them to say, will always deliver the same message: These "Ahl al Bayt", divinely pure, created flawless, stand above all, created under the eternal light of Allah.

Regrettably, many Ahadith and histories were compiled 80 to two hundred years after the passing of the prophet of Islam. The totalitarian and despotic regimes of Umayyads and Abbasids have, for 300 years, methodically undermined facts and covered their tracks with fabricated Ahadith.

To identify the fake material, one has to apply the rule that Muhammad gave: accept only those Ahadith that agree with Quran. Any conflict with authentic Ahadith of Muhammad must be discarded. Who is better in the interpretation of Quran than Muhammad? His word cannot be challenged because Allah defines Muhammad in Quran:

وَمَا يَنطِقُ عَنِ الْهَوَى

*And neither does he speak out of his own desire: 53:3* **(Asad)**

إِنْ هُوَ إِلَّا وَحْيٌ يُوحَى

*That [which he conveys to you] is but [a divine] inspiration with which he is being inspired. 53:4* **(Asad)**

The analyses done on this verse to this point proves beyond any shadow of doubt that the "Ahl al Bayt" are none other than Muhammad, Ali, Fatimah, Hasan and Husayn.

A true Muslim is bound by the commands of Allah to accept every word Muhammad had said, if they wish to remain a Muslim. It would be sacrilegious for any Mufasir (exegete) or scholar to contradict Muhammad about the identity "Ahl al Bayt" in "Aya Tatheer".

The following conclusions are drawn after intensely scrutinizing over 1400 years of data pertaining to this subject matter:

1.  It has been established that Muhammad's final ruling about the identity of "Ahl al Bayt" in "Aya Tatheer" was about none other than Fatimah, Ali, Hasan and Husayn. This was further reinforced when Muhammad, pointing at Fatimah, Ali, Hasan and Husayn said, "Ha Ulai Ahl al Bayt" (These are my Ahl al Bayt).

2.  It is a fact that Allah has never addressed the wives of Muhammad as "Ahl al Bayt" anywhere in Quran.

3.  If the wives were any part of "Aya Tatheer", the verse would have been in a feminine plural form. Since "Aya Tatheer" is in masculine plural gender, any possibility to include the wives in this verse is eliminated.

4.  "*Buyutekunna*" was specifically used in verse 33 and 34 to demonstrate that there were several houses (*Buyutekunna*) that Muhammad's wives lived in. By specifically linking the term "*Buyutekunna*" with the wives of Muhammad, Allah was creating the distinction between "ahl al Bayt" (referring to a selective single household) and the wives of Muhammad. Furthermore, since the term "*Buyutekunna*" was not used in "Aya Tatheer" in place of "Ahl al Bayt" to address multiple houses, any possibility of including his wives is eliminated.

5.  There is no hadith about Muhammad ever saying that the term "Ahl al Bayt" in verse 33 was about his wives.

6.  An interesting point to note is that none of his wives ever claimed that the term "Ahl al Bayt" in "Aya Tatheer" was about them.

7.  It has been demonstrated that Umm Salama and Aiysha failed to get permission from Muhammad to become a part of the *"Kisa"*. They both expressed their inability to become part of "Ahl al Bayt" in this verse.

8.  The fact that two of Muhammad's wives misbehaved and were threatened by divorce in Quran disqualifies them from the terms *"Yutahhirakum Tatheerah"* and "Ahl al Bayt". Their disobedience to Muhammad and Allah was enough to put them in violation of the attribute of purity and spotlessness guaranteed in "Aya Tatheer".

9.  The most important fact often ignored is that Um Salam and Aiysha asked permission to be part of "Ahl al Bayt" **after** "Aya Tatheer" had **already** been revealed to Muhammad, Ali Fatimah, Hasan and Husayn under the "Kisa" mantle. Once the verse was delivered without the wives under the "Kisa" cover, it is technically impossible to include them as part of the "Ahl al Bayt".

10. Two powerful proceedings where Muhammad openly declared his "Ahl al Bayt" as Fatimah, Ali, Hasan and Husayn are "Mubahala" and "Aya Mawaddah". These declarations are solid proofs about the identity of the "Ahl al Bayt".

11. Muhammad, according to his companions and relatives, declared that his "Ahl al Bayt" are Ali, Fatimah, Hasan and Husayn. Muhammad, for up to 9 months prior to his passing away, made it his practice to go to Fatimah's home every day, call for prayer time, and recite the "Aya Tatheer" addressing Fatimah's family.

12. The most compelling testimonial is the analysis of each word of "Aya Tatheer" presented in chapter 7. The setup of the words so carefully strung together

makes it impossible to include anyone into the term "Ahl al Bayt" besides Muhammad, Fatimah, Ali, Hasan and Husayn. The three syllables in "Ahl al Bayt" describe who can be part of the term "Ahl al Bayt". The part "al Bayt" narrows it down to **only one special household**.

13. Significant change in the language and tone between "Aya Tatheer" and the seven verses around it exacerbates the split between the groups being described. The change from harsh and punitive language in verses 28 - 33, to honor, respect, and mercy only in "Aya Tatheer" indicate that two characteristically different groups of people are being addressed. The structure of "Aya Tatheer" is all praises and gratification for creating a chosen group with the highest level of moral and ethical exactitude.

The above list of a minimum of 13 proofs have been presented to demonstrate that "Ahl al Bayt" in verse 33 of Surah Ahzab represent none other than Muhammad, Ali, Fatimah, Hasan and Husayn.

A majority of Islamic scholars agree that the "Ahl al Bayt" in this verse represents the five individuals mentioned above. Some of the adversaries of Muhammad, Fatimah, Ali, Hasan and Husayn have tried and failed to include Muhammad's wives and relatives.

The last and the most crucial point previously discussed that a believer must focus on is the individual making the point. Of course, the words of Allah and Muhammad supersede the words of Mufasereen (exegetes), interpreters, and Muhaditheen(traditionalists).

وَمَا يَنطِقُ عَنِ الْهَوَى ۚ إِنْ هُوَ إِلَّا وَحْيٌ يُوحَى

*Wama yantiqu AAani alhawa | In huwa illa wahyun yooha*

*and neither does he speak out of his own desire: – 53:3 **(Asad)**. that [which he conveys to you] is but [a divine] inspiration with which he is being inspired – – 53:4 **(Asad)***

If Muhammad, the divine representative, has pointed at Fatimah, Ali, Hasan and Husayn and said "*Ha ulai Ahl al Bayt*" (These are my Ahl al Bayt), then it would be catastrophic to one's faith to challenge Muhammad.

Every scenario was examined in depth by purely logical reasoning. Fictitious constituents were identified and weeded out. "Haqq" remained the focal point throughout the development of this book.

It has been demonstrated beyond any doubt from the Quran, Hadith, Tafseer and history, that the term "Ahl al Bayt" in "Aya Tatheer", verse 33 of Surah Ahzab, is **only** about Muhammad, Ali, Fatimah, Hasan and Husayn.

I conclude this book with the words of the Quran, and the incumbency it places upon its believers to stand up for "Haqq".

وَمَا كَانَ لِمُؤْمِنٍ وَلَا مُؤْمِنَةٍ إِذَا قَضَى اللَّهُ وَرَسُولُهُ أَمْرًا أَن يَكُونَ لَهُمُ الْخِيَرَةُ

مِنْ أَمْرِهِمْ وَمَن يَعْصِ اللَّهَ وَرَسُولَهُ فَقَدْ ضَلَّ ضَلَالًا مُّبِينًا

*Now whenever God and His Apostle have decided a matter, it is not for a believing man or a believing woman to claim freedom of choice insofar as they themselves are concerned: for he who [thus] rebels against God and His Apostle has already, most obviously, gone astray. 33:36 **(Asad)***

# Notes

Chapter 3

## Note 1

### "Kisa"

A "kisa" is a mantle or cloak that Prophet Muhammad had repeatedly used to cover himself, Ali, Fatimah, Hassan and Husayn prior to the revelation of "Aya Tatheer". This enclosure was created to establish the boundaries of the revelation that was to be revealed inside the canopy of "Kisa". Each member entered under the "kisa" with Muhammad, as he prepared for the revelation to come. When all five members had gathered under the "kisa", the archangel Gabriel asked for permission to enter. He was granted permission by Allah to enter the Kisa to deliver the "Aya Tatheer". Gabriel proclaimed: "Allah's only intention is to keep away all abominations only from you O' 'Ahl al Bayt' and to keep you pure and spotless", addressing those who were under the mantle.

There were at least two wives who witnessed this event. If there was no "kisa" canopy and if Gabriel had delivered the verse outside of the "kisa" it would have included Umm Salama (everyone) in that room. The fact that the verse was delivered inside the "kisa" canopy eliminated the possibility of including others who may have been present in that room. Umm Salama and Aiysha realized the importance of being within the confines of the "kisa". They asked permission to enter and were denied entry into the "kisa" as discussed in earlier chapters.

The authenticity of this hadith is well established. The following is a shot list of references:

1.  Minhaaj Al Sunnah – Volume 3, page 3; Sahih Tirmidhi – Volume 5, page 351, Hadeeth # 3105; Hakim

2.  Al Nisapouri (Mustadrak Al Sahihain) – Volume 3, page 146); Sahih Muslim – Volume 4, page 1883, Hadeeth # 2424; Masnad Ahmad ibn Hanbal – Volume 6, page 292

3.  Narrator: Ibn Abbas:
    Ahmad ibn Hanbal (Al Masnad) – Volume 1, page 331; Ibn Abi 'Asem (Al Sunnah) – Volume 2, page 602, Hadeeth 1351; Al Nisaai (Al Sunan Al Kubra) – Volume 5, page 112, Hadeeth 8409; Al Tabrani (Mu'jam Al Kabir) – Volume 12, page 77, Hadeeth # 12593; Al Hakim (Al Mustadrak) – Volume 3, page 133.

4.  Narrator: Umm Salama:

    Abu Al Shaykh (Tabaqaat Al Muhaditheen) – Volume 4, page 149, Hadeeth #
    915; Al Khatib (Al Mutafaq Wal Muftaraq) – Volume 2, page 11588, Hadeeth
    # 723; Ibn A'saker (Tarikh) – Volume 42, page 136, Hadeeth # 8518.

5.  Narrator: A'yesha bint Abi Bakr:

    Ibn Abi Shayba (Al Mussanaf) – Volume 6, page 373, Hadeeth # 32093;
    Muslim (Al Jame'a Al Sahih) – Volume 2, page 283, Hadeeth 2424; Al Hakim
    (Al Mustadrak) – Volume 3, page 147.

Chapter 4:

# Note 1

## ANFUSANA

فَمَنْ حَآجَّكَ فِيهِ مِن بَعْدِ مَا جَاءكَ مِنَ الْعِلْمِ فَقُلْ تَعَالَوْاْ نَدْعُ أَبْنَاءنَا وَأَبْنَاءكُمْ

وَنِسَاءنَا وَنِسَاءكُمْ وَأَنفُسَنَا وأَنفُسَكُمْ ثُمَّ نَبْتَهِلْ فَنَجْعَل لَّعْنَةُ اللهِ عَلَى الْكَاذِبِينَ

*If any one disputes in this matter with thee, now after (full) knowledge Hath come to
thee, say: "Come! let us gather together,- our sons and your sons, our women and your
women, ourselves and yourselves: Then let us earnestly pray, and invoke the curse of
Allah on those who lie!" (3:61).*

The term "anfusana", which is usually defined as "selves", appears generic. The term carries with it, in relation to Muhammad, a much greater and deeper meaning. With "anfusana" it is understood that Muhammad has brought with him someone of the same stature and distinction. Because the term "anfusana" is in the plural form, Muhammad could have taken other personalities with him as well, but he chose to take only Ali with him, because Ali was declared by Surah Ahzab, verse 33, as pure and spotless.

Muhammad said that "Ali is from me and I am from Ali".[1] One example that demonstrates the congruency of these two personalities is the case of the announcement of the verses of surah Barah by the Kaabah: The verses, which relate to the prohibition of the idolaters from entering Kaabah (house of Allah), circumambulating Kaabah without clothes, and dishonoring their pact (The Treaty of Suleh Hudaibiyah) with Muslims, were initially given to Abu Bakr from Surah Barah for public announcement. He was on his way to Kaabah to recite these verses, when Muhammad received a revelation from Allah ordering him to have these verses be read either by him (Muhammad) or someone from him (someone of his stature). Muhammad called Ali and ordered him to stop Abu Bakr and take over the responsibility of reciting the verses of Sura Barah (also known as surah Tawbah). Ali took over the task from Abu Bakr and delivered the verses at Kaabah among the enemies of Islam. A disappointed Abu Bakr approached Muhammad and asked him what had brought about this change. Muhammad said it was the revelation which he received from Allah ordering the change in assignment of the mission to be completed only by him (Muhammad) or someone like him.[2,3]

(1) Ibn Hanbal's Musnad, Mtba'ah Al-Maymaniyyah, Vol 4, PP. 164-165, 1st edition, Egypt 1313 AH.

(2) Ibn Hanbal's Musnad, Mtba'ah Al-Maymaniyyah, Vol 4, PP. 164-165, 1st edition, Egypt 1313 AH.

(3) Ibn Ishaq. The Life of Muhammad. Translator A. Guillaume, Oxford Press. 1967, p 619.

## Note 2

### Ghadir e Khumm

This event dramatically changed the history of Islam. The Islamic world would have reached perfection if the believers had followed the orders from the Almighty God at "Ghadir e Khumm". The highlight of Muhammad's success of the completion of his assigned task depended on the delivery of one of the most important message from Allah. This announcement about Ali's position, and his mission on the grounds of "Ghadir e Khumm", was so crucial that it had to be strategically enshrined between two verses of the Quran. Allah deliberately made the acceptance of Muhammad's mission contingent upon the declaration of Ali's role after Muhammad.

The significance of this event is reflected from the circumstances and conditions under which Muhammad was ordered by the Almighty Allah to deliver this crucial message to the believers with a warning (5:67) to Muhammad that if he did not, it would demolish all of the work he had done as the prophet of Islam.

يَا أَيُّهَا الرَّسُولُ بَلِّغْ مَا أُنزِلَ إِلَيْكَ مِن رَّبِّكَ وَإِن لَّمْ تَفْعَلْ فَمَا بَلَّغْتَ رِسَالَتَهُ وَاللّهُ يَعْصِمُكَ

مِنَ النَّاسِ إِنَّ اللّهَ لاَ يَهْدِي الْقَوْمَ الْكَافِرِينَ

*O Messenger! proclaim the (message) which hath been sent to thee from thy Lord. If thou didst not, thou wouldst not have fulfilled and proclaimed His mission. And Allah will defend thee from men (who mean mischief). For Allah guideth not those who reject Faith (5:67).*

Muhammad, among thousands (100,000 -125,000) of returning pilgrims from his last Hajj stopped at a crucial juncture, created a stage, and as commanded by Allah declared:

*"Man kunto maula fa haza Ali un maula"*

*"Whomever I am his master, this Ali is his master" (1).*

This historic declaration was unique, and its aim was to consolidate and safeguard the future of Islam under the guardianship of Ali.

Muhammad stopped at Ghadir e Khumm under the harshest conditions, built a stage, and delivered a lengthy sermon to the thousands, then lifted Ali's hands and said "Man kunto Maula fa hasa Ali un Maula", then asked the attendees who had pledged their allegiance to him and to Islam, to also pledge their allegiance to Ali (2). Among the thousands who pledged their allegiance to Ali were, notably, Abu Bakr, Umar, and Usman (3).

The unfolding of the events at "Ghadir e Khumm" suggests that Muhammad had put thousands of believers through difficulties to build a special stage at a critical juncture under heat and exhaustion to declare himself and Ali in a commanding position as a "guardian" and a "leader" and not merely a "friend" to the community, as some muhaditheen have suggested.

Muhammad took an extraordinary step to deconvolute and define the meaning of the term "Maula" by ordering the believers to pledge their allegiance to Ali (2). Quran in its own intrepid and subtle way characterizes allegiance in the following verse:

إِنَّ الَّذِينَ يُبَايِعُونَكَ إِنَّمَا يُبَايِعُونَ اللَّهَ يَدُ اللَّهِ فَوْقَ أَيْدِيهِمْ فَمَن نَّكَثَ فَإِنَّمَا يَنكُثُ

عَلَى نَفْسِهِ وَمَنْ أَوْفَى بِمَا عَاهَدَ عَلَيْهُ اللَّهَ فَسَيُؤْتِيهِ أَجْرًا عَظِيمًا

*Lo! those who swear allegiance unto thee (Muhammad), swear allegiance only unto Allah. The Hand of Allah is above their hands. So, whosoever breaketh his oath, breaketh it only to his soul's hurt; while whosoever keepeth his covenant with Allah, on him will He bestow immense reward. - 48:10* **(Picktall)**

Allegiance to Muhammad under the supreme authority of Allah in the above verse establishes the authority and administrative leadership of Muhammad and disobedience to Muhammad is considered disobedience to Allah. Allegiance is defined as loyalty, of a subject to his sovereign, or loyalty of a citizen to his country. By ordering allegiance to Ali, Muhammad was defining the term "Maula" as "master, guardian, custodian". It would be naïve for muhaditheen to consider that the term "Maula" was intended to declare Ali simply as a "friend".

Allah's declaration of perfecting the religion of Islam came after the announcement of "Mun Kunto Maula fa haza Aliun Maula" when Allah accepted the completion of Muhammad's mission at Ghadir e Khumm:

الْيَوْمَ أَكْمَلْتُ لَكُمْ دِينَكُمْ وَأَتْمَمْتُ عَلَيْكُمْ نِعْمَتِي وَرَضِيتُ لَكُمُ الإِسْلاَمَ دِينًا

*This day have I perfected your religion for you, completed My favour upon you, and have chosen for you Islam as your religion (5:3).*

To recapitulate the events at Ghadir e Khumm:

1.  Allah ordered Muhammad to announce the completion of his mission:

يَا أَيُّهَا الرَّسُولُ بَلِّغْ مَا أُنزِلَ إِلَيْكَ مِن رَّبِّكَ وَإِن لَّمْ تَفْعَلْ فَمَا بَلَّغْتَ رِسَالَتَهُ وَاللّهُ

يَعْصِمُكَ مِنَ النَّاسِ إِنَّ اللّهَ لاَ يَهْدِي الْقَوْمَ الْكَافِرِينَ

*O Messenger! proclaim the (message) which hath been sent to thee from thy Lord. If thou didst not, thou wouldst not have fulfilled and proclaimed His mission. And <u>Allah</u> will* *defend thee from men (who mean mischief). For Allah guideth not those who reject Faith (5:67).*

2. Muhammad responded by preparing the stage and declaring:

*"Man kunto maula fa haza Ali un maula". "Whomever I am his master, this Ali is his master" (1).*

3. Allah followed it by his own statement accepting and celebrating the completion of Muhammad's mission:

$$اليَوْمَ أَكْمَلْتُ لَكُمْ دِينَكُمْ وَأَتْمَمْتُ عَلَيْكُمْ نِعْمَتِي وَرَضِيتُ لَكُمُ الإِسْلاَمَ دِينًا$$

*This day have I perfected your religion for you, completed My favour upon you, and have chosen for you Islam as your religion (5:3).*

4. Muhammad culminated the day by asking the community to pledge allegiance to Ali.

The event of "Ghadir e Khumm" itself is undeniably recognized on a bipartisan basis. The term Maula is therefore about a leader, a guardian, an administrator, and an authority on Islam and implementor of the Islamic laws.

Numerous speeches, articles and books has been written on this important event. The book by Amini titled "*Al-Ghadir - fi l-kitāb wa l-sunna wa l-adab*" recently translated into Urdu language is highly detailed and thoroughly researched. This is incontestably the best book on "Ghadir e Khumm" with additional discussions on various related material (4).

References:

1.  Musnad Ahmad Hanbal, Chapter 39, Pg 297, Hadith 18497

2.  Sahih Tirmidhi, v2, p298, v5, p63; Sunan Ibn Maja, v1, pp 12,43; Khasa'is, by al-Nisa'i, pp 4,21; al-Mustadrak, by al-Hakim, v2, p129, v3, pp 109-110, 116,371; Musnad Ahmad Ibn Hanbal, v1, pp 84).

3.  Musnad Ahmad Ibn Hanbal, v4, p281;Tafsir al-Kabir, by Fakhr al-Razi, v12, pp 49-50.

4.  Al Ghadir, by Abdul Hussain Amini Najafi, 1995. Urdu Translation by Syed Ali Akhtar Rizvi, 2012.

# Note 3

## Da'wat dhu 'l-'Ashira

Muhammad had been interactively practicing Islam from the very beginning of his life, and about three years after he received the first revelation of Quran he was ordered to reveal the message of Islam to the world:

$$وَأَنذِرْ عَشِيرَتَكَ الْأَقْرَبِينَ$$

And warn thy tribe of near kindred, - 26:214 **(Picktall)**

Ali and his father Abu Talib arranged a feast for their relatives to help Muhammad spread the word of Allah. Before Muhammad could present the message of Islam, one of his uncles named Abu Lahab, who was openly against this new religion that Muhammad was about to present, sabotaged the meeting and undermined the movement. People dispersed, and Muhammad's first attempt was aborted. The feast was rearranged on the second day and Muhammad took the center stage and announced:

'O children of Abd al-Muttalib,' cried he (Mohammed) with enthusiasm, 'to you, of all men, has Allah vouchsafed these most precious gifts. In his name I offer you the blessings of this world, and endless joys hereafter. Who among you will share the burden of my offer? Who will be my brother, my lieutenant, my vizir (vicegerent) ?' All remained silent; some wondering; others smiling with incredulity and derision. At length Ali, starting up with youthful zeal, offered himself to the service of the Prophet though modestly acknowledging his youth and physical weakness. Mohammed threw up his arms around the generous youth, and pressed him to his bosom. 'Behold my brother, my vizir, my vicegerent,' exclaimed he, "Let all listen to his words, and obey him". (Reference : The Life of Mohammed by Washington Irving).

According to a second source concerning the unfolding of the events at Da'wat dhu 'l-'Ashira:

Muhammad said; "Which of you will aid me in this matter, so that he will be my brother, my agent (wasi) and my successor (Khalifah) among you?"

Ali repeated his commitment again on the second day and Muhammad reiterated acceptance of Ali's support by declaring:

"This is my brother, my agent, and my successor among you, so listen to him and obey him." - History of al-Tabari v. 6, Muhammad at Mecca, State University of New York press, translated by W.Montgomery Watt amd M.V. McDonald. 1988. Page 90-91.

Chapter 6

# Note 1

## Wilayat

surah Maidah verse 55

إِنَّمَا وَلِيُّكُمُ اللّٰهُ وَرَسُولُهُ وَالَّذِينَ آمَنُواْ الَّذِينَ يُقِيمُونَ الصَّلَاةَ وَيُؤْتُونَ

الزَّكَاةَ وَهُمْ رَاكِعُونَ

*Innama valiyu kum allah wa rasoolahu wallazina amanul lazina yoqemunas salata wa you tunas zakata wa hum raki oon.*

*No one except Allah is your "Wali" and His Messenger and those who believe, those who keep up prayers and pay the poor-rate **while** they bow.*

There are numerous translations of the word "Wali". Broadly speaking it can take the meaning of helper, friend, assistant, confederate, son-in-law, leader, and master. The semantics and more importantly the context in which these terms are used determines their purpose and meaning.

Unfortunately, the following verse is usually quoted by some exegetes to create unnecessary confusion between the term "Awlia", which is translated as "friends" in verse 51, in contrast to Allah referring to Himself as "Wali" to reflect his authority and guardianship over mankind in verse 55.

يَا أَيُّهَا الَّذِينَ آمَنُواْ لاَ تَتَّخِذُواْ الْيَهُودَ وَالنَّصَارَى أَوْلِيَاء بَعْضُهُمْ أَوْلِيَاء بَعْضٍ

وَمَن يَتَوَلَّهُم مِّنكُمْ فَإِنَّهُ مِنْهُمْ إِنَّ اللهَ لاَ يَهْدِي الْقَوْمَ الظَّالِمِينَ

*O YOU who have attained to faith! Do not take the Jews and the Christians for your friends (Awlia): they are but friends of one another and whoever of you friends himself with them becomes, verily, one of them; behold, God does not guide such evildoers. 5:51 **(Asad)***

There are glaring differences between the usage of the term "Awlia" in verse 51 and "Wali" in verse 55. The word "Awlia" in verse 51 is to pronounce the relationship between the Jews and Christians as friends for their collaborative activities that Allah considered hostile towards the believers.

Verse 51 is a warning to the believers not to make friends/allies with the Jews and Christians in this situation, and that if they do make friends with them they will be considered evildoers. The hostile conditions in this instance created by the Jews and Christians is the main reason for caution. It is important to note that the word used "Awlia" in verse 51 is specific to describe the friendship or collusion between two groups.

In contrast, the terms "Wali" and "Wilayat" are about authority and guardianship. The term "Wali" and its derivative "Wilayat" has many dimensions. Both terms have deep meaning and serve the purpose of proving guidance, direction and spiritual leadership to a believer. The word "Wali" in verse 55 is used in a significantly different setting. "Wali" here refers to the Wilayat of Allah, and the context in which it is used serves the purpose of recognizing the authoritative guidance Allah provides to all mankind. This guidance transcends through Muhammad and Ali as declared in verse 55. "Innama waliyo kumallahu" is translated as "Only Allah is your Wali". The word "Wali' is strategically enclosed between "Innama" and "Allah" to deliver authoritative memorandum. Therefore, the proper translation that will correspond to Allah's supreme being would be "Master" or "Guardian". Allah is "Wali" and Muhammad, on Allah's authority, is granted the position of "Wilayat" in the same context, and it is further extended down the line to the "Wilayat" of Ali in recognition of the act of compassion displayed by him when he gave away his ring to uphold one of the core principles of Islam. Allah is basically establishing the authority of Muhammad and Ali over the mankind.

Ali was an embodiment of compassion, mercy, love and justice. He rose above the brutal trials and tribulations he and his family faced and demonstrated their commitment to support and advance the message of Islam in the most extraordinary circumstances. Allah recognized his love for Islam and honored him with "Wilayat".

Chapter 7

## Note 1

## Masoom

$$وَمَا أَرْسَلْنَا مِن رَّسُولٍ إِلاَّ لِيُطَاعَ بِإِذْنِ اللّهِ$$

*"And we did not send any messenger, unless he should be obeyed by Allah's authority."(Qur'an 4:64)*

The concept of a Masoom is that he or she does not under any circumstance commit any sin even though he or she is able to. The Masooms, selected by Allah has total freedom but their moral obligations prevent them from committing any sin. These messengers are Allah's viceroys and human models for humanity. They are to present themselves as humans with ideal moral and ethical integrity and outstanding character. There will be no point in sending an unreliable messengers with flawed background to preach and propagate an ideal way of life outlined in Islam. It was important to send a messenger who would practice and preach justice, peace, freedom, love, respect to fellow beings and compassion. Muhammad the last messenger had all the elements necessary to present and propagate a perfect religion, Islam.

وَمَا آتَاكُمُ الرَّسُولُ فَخُذُوهُ وَمَا نَهَاكُمْ عَنْهُ فَانتَهُوا

*"And whatever the Messenger gives you, take it; and from whatever he forbids you, keep back."(Qur'an 59:7)*

The creator has to be pure, perfect and flawless in selection of his messenger. Muhammad a perfect model endorsed by Allah was delivered and the believers were expected to obey him on Allah's authority. Allah's command to take whatever Muhammad gives and to reject whatever he forbids, defines the confidence that Allah has in Muhammad's decisions in any task.

مَا ضَلَّ صَاحِبُكُمْ وَمَا غَوَى

*Your companion (i.e., Prophet) does not err/wander, nor is he deceived (Qur'an 53:2)*

The above verse clearly declares that Muhammad does not stumble. He is neither misled or defrauded.

وَمَا يَنطِقُ عَنِ الْهَوَى

*Nor does he speak out of his desire; (Qur'an 53:3)*

إِنْ هُوَ إِلَّا وَحْيٌ يُوحَى

*It is no less than a revelation that is revealed. (Qur'an 53:4)*

The above two verses provide assurance that Muhammad does not speak or convey anything to the mankind unless endorsed by Allah.

And finally, the verse "Aya Tatheer" is an ultimate guarantee that Muhammad is pure and flawless and unquestionably a masoom.

# References

Introduction

1. - The Prophet (S) said to 'Ali: "You are from me, and I am from you".
   Sahih al-Bukhari, Arabic-English version, v5, Tradition 553.

   - The Messenger of Allah said: "Husayn is from me and I am from al-Husayn."

   Musnad Ahmad Ibn Hanbal, v4, p172; Fadha'il al-Sahaba, by Ahmad

   Hanbal, v2, p772, Tradition 1361; al-Mustadrak, by al-Hakim, v3, p177;

   Amali, by Abu Nu'aym al-Isbahani, p64; al-Kuna wal Asmaa, by al-Dulabi,

   v1, p88; al-Tabarani, v3, p21; al-Sawa'iq al-Muhriqah, by Ibn Hajar

   Haythami, Ch. 11, section 3, p291; Mishkat al-Masabih, by Khatib al-Tabrizi,

   English Version, Tradition 6160;

   - Miswar bin Makhramah (ra) narrates that the Messenger of Allah (saw) said,

   "Fatimah is a part of me. Therefore, whosoever angers her angers me.";

   Bukhari, as-Sahih 3:1361#3510; Bukhari, as-Sahih 3:1374#3556; Muslim,

   as-Sahih 4:1903#2449.

- Jabir bin Abdullah (ra) narrates that the Holy Prophet (saw) said, "It is the father that every woman's children are attributed to, except for Fatimah's sons. I am their guardian and I am their lineage."

Hakim, al-Mustadrak 3:169,170#4739, 4740.

Chapter 1

1. Abul Ala Maududi, Tafheem e Quran, surah Ahzab verse 33.

Chapter 3

1. Sahih Bukhari, Volume 3, Book 43, Number 648; Sahih Bukhari 6:438; Sahih Bukhari 6:436; Sahih Bukhari 7:119; Sahih Bukhari 4:435.

2. Abul Ala Maududi, Tafheem e Quran, surah Ahzab verse 33.

3. Barbara F. Stowasser, Women in Quran, Traditions, and interpretation, Oxford University press, 1994, pages 59-60; Christopher P. Clohessy, Fatimah, Daughter of Muhammad, Gorgis press, 2009, page 57; Sahih al Tirmidi V5, Page 135; Al Hakim, Al Mustadrak V3, Page 157; Ahmad Ibn Hanbal, Musnad V3, Page 135.

4. Sahih al-Tirmidhi, v5, pp 351,663.

5. al-Durr al-Manthoor, by al-Hafidh al-Suyuti, v5, p198.

6. Abul Ala Maududi, Tafheem e Quran, Surah Ahzab verse 33.

7. Tahawi Hanafi, Mushkil Al-Athar, Vol 1, PP 332-339. (verify)

8. Quran Tafsir Ibn Kathir, Surah Ahzab verse 33.

9. Al Kashaf, by Al Dhahabi, v2, p272

Chapter 4

1. Sahih al-Tirmidhi, v5, pp 351,663.

2. al-Mustadrak, by al-Hakim, v2, p416

3. Usdul Ghabah, by Ibn al-Athir, v2, p289.

4. Tafsir al-Durr al-Manthoor, by al-Suyuti, v5, p198.

5. Tafsir al-Tabari, v22, p7 under the commentary of verse 33:33.

6. al-Mustadrak by al-Hakim, Chapter of "Understanding (the virtues) of Companions, v3, p148.

7. Talkhis of al-Mustadrak, by al-Dhahabi, v3, p148

8. Usdul Ghabah, by Ibn al-Athir, v3, p33.

9. Sahih Muslim, Chapter of virtues of companions, section of the virtues of the Ahlul-Bayt of the Prophet (S), 1980 Edition Pub. in Saudi Arabia, Arabic version, v4, p1883, Tradition #61.

10. Sahih al-Tirmidhi, v12, p85, Musnad Ahmad Ibn Hanbal, v3, p258, Mustadrak, by al-Hakim,v3, p158, Tafsir al-Durr al-Manthoor, by al-Suyuti, v5, pp 197,199, Tafsir Ibn Jarir al-Tabari, v22, pp 5,6 (saying seven month), Tafsir Ibn Kathir, v3, p483, Musnad, by al-Tiyalasi, v8, p274, Usdul Ghabah, by Ibn al-Athir, v5, p146

11. Tafsir al-Durr al-Manthoor, by al-Suyuti, v5, pp 198-199, Tafsir Ibn Jarir al-Tabari, v22, p6, Tafsir Ibn Kathir, v3, p483, Dhakha'ir al-Uqba, by Muhibbuddin al-Tabari, p24 on the authority of Anas Ibn Malik, Isti'ab, by Ibn Abd al-Barr, v5, p637, Usdul Ghabah, by Ibn al-Athir, v5, p146, Majma' al-Zawa'id, by al-Haythami, v9, pp 121,168, Mushkil al-Athar, by al-Tahawi, p338.

12. al-Durr al-Manthoor, by al-Hafidh al-Suyuti, v5, p198.

13. Tafsir al-Durr al-Manthoor, by al-Hafidh al-Suyuti, v5, p199, Majma' al-Zawa'id, by al-Haythami, v9, pp 121,168.

14. Tafsir al-Kabir, by Ibn Jarir al-Tabari, v22, p7, Tafsir Ibn Kathir, v3, p485, al-Mustadrak, by al-Hakim, v3, p147, Mushkil al-Athar, by al-Tahawi, v1, p336; v2, p33, History of al-Tabari, Arabic version, v5, p31.

15. Tafsir Ibn Jarir al-Tabari, v22, p5, under the verse 33:33, Dhakha'ir al-Uqba, Muhibbuddin al-Tabari, p24, al-Sawa'iq al-Muhriqah, by Ibn Hajar, Ch. 11, section 1, p221, Majma' al-Zawa'id, by al-Haythami.

16. Tafsir al-Kabir, by Ibn Jarir al-Tabari, v22, p6, al-Mustadrak, by al-Hakim, v2, p416; v3, p417, Musnad, by Ahmad Ibn Hanbal, v6, p107, Majma' al-Zawa'id, by al-Haythami, v9, p167, Mushkil al-Athar, by al-Tahawi, v1, p346, Sunan, al-Bayhaqqi, v2, p152.

17. Usdul Ghabah, by Ibn al-Athir, v2, p20.

18. Ibrahim Al Qunduzi in "Yanabi al Mawaddah", chapter 33, page 168

19. Al-Durr al-Manthoor by al-Hafidh Jalaluddin al-Suyuti, v2, p38

20. Sahih Muslim, Chapter of virtues of companions, section of virtues of 'Ali, 1980 Edition Pub. in Saudi Arabia, Arabic version, v4, p1871, the end of tradition #32., Sahih al-Tirmidhi, v5, p654, al-Mustadrak, by al-Hakim, v3, p150, who said this tradition is authentic based on the criteria set by two Shaikhs, al-Bukhari and Muslim., 'Dhakha'ir al-Uqba' Muhibbuddin al-Tabari, p25.

21. Tafsir al-Kabir, by Fakhr al-Din al-Razi, Part 27, pp 165-166., Tafsir al-Tha'labi, under the commentary of verse 42:23 of Quran., Tafsir al-Tabari, by Ibn Jarir al- Tabari, under verse 42:23., Tafsir al-Qurtubi, under commentary of verse 42:23 of Quran., Tafsir al-Kashshaf, by al-Zamakhshari, under commentary of verse 42:23., Tafsir al-Baidhawi, under the commentary of verse 42:23 of Quran., al-Madarik, in connection with verse 42:23., Dhakha'ir al-Uqba, by Muhibbuddin al-Tabari, p25., Musnad Ahmad Ibn Hanbal, "Manaqib" p110., al-Sawa'iq al-Muhriqah, by Ibn Hajar Haythami, Ch. 11, section 1, p259., Shawahid al-Tanzeel, Hakim Hasakani, al-Hanafi, v2, p132.

22. Madelung, The Succession to Muhammad, p. 14-15 (21)

23. "Fāṭima". Encyclopaedia of Islam, Second Edition. Edited by: P. Bearman, Th. Bianquis, C.E. Bosworth, E. van Donzel, W.P. Heinrichs. Brill Online, 2014. Reference. 08 April 2014.

24. at Tabari, at-Ta'rikh, vol. 1 (Leiden, 1980 offset of the 1789 edition) p. 171-173; Ibn al-Athir, al-Kamil, vol. 5 (Beirut, 1965) p. 62-63; Abu 'l-Fida', al-Mukhtasar fi Ta'rikhi 'l-Bashar, vol. 1 (Beirut, n.d.) p. 116-117; al-Khazin, at-Tafsir, vol. 4 (Cairo, 1955) p. 127; al-Baghawi, at-Tafsir (Ma'alimu 't-Tanzil),

vol. 6 (Riyadh: Dar Tayyiba, 1993) p. 131; al-Bayhaqi, Dala'ilu 'nNubuwwa, vol. 1 (Cairo, 1969) p. 428-430; as-Suyuti, ad-Durru 'l-Manthur, vol. 5 (Beirut, n.d.) p. 97; and Muttaqi al-Hindi, Kanzu 'l-'Ummal, vol. 15 (Hyderabad, 1968) pp. 100, 113, 115. For further references, see 'Abdu 'l-Husayn al-Amini, alGhadir, vol. 2 (Beirut, 1967) pp. 278-289. In English see, Rizvi, S. Saeed Akhtar, Imamate: the Vicegerency of the Prophet (Tehran: WOFIS, 1985) pp. 57-60.

25. Ibn Ishaq; Translation by A. Gilllaume; The Life of Muhammad; Oxford University Press 1967 p118.

26. Al-Bukhari in his Sahih part 6 p. 3.

27. Musnad Ahmad Hanbal, Chapter 39, Pg 297, Hadith 18497

28. Sahih Tirmidhi, v2, p298, v5, p63; Sunan Ibn Maja, v1, pp 12,43; Khasa'is, by al-Nisa'i, pp 4,21; al-Mustadrak, by al-Hakim, v2, p129, v3, pp 109-110, 116,371; Musnad Ahmad Ibn Hanbal, v1, pp 84).

29. Musnad Ahmad Ibn Hanbal, v4, p281;Tafsir al-Kabir, by Fakhr al-Razi, v12, pp 49-50.

# Acknowledgement

I would like to thank Allah for providing me parents who structured my life on the path of Muhammad and Aal-e-Muhammad. My parents, Syed Muhammad Jafer Rizvi and Yousuf Zehra Begum Rizvi, were a guiding light in my understanding of Islam. They helped me to recognize and cherish the role played by the Ahl al Bayt AS to preserve and propagate Islam. They encouraged me to be unshakable in standing up for truth.

I would like to thank the Ulema/scholars who helped me understand the importance of this project. I also would like to acknowledge the fifty-year-old lecture by Maulana Ali Naqui that was made available to me, where he discussed the grammar and semantics of "Aya Tatheer". The lecture of Maulana Sheikh Muhammad Al Hilli and Maulana Sheikh Mateen Charbonneau regarding the interpretation of each word in "Aya Tatheer" were extremely helpful. I had lengthy discussion about this verse with Maulana Muntazir Mehdi. My brief discussions with Dr. Salman Turabi and Maulana Mehboob Mehdi were extremely helpful. The highlighted words from the seven verses around the "Aya Tatheer" relating to the gender modulations were adopted from the presentation of a video of Maulana Syed Muhammad Rizvi.

I would like to thank my son Syed Khasim Taqui Rizvi for his priceless suggestions in structuring the layout of various chapters. Khasim is primarily responsible for the editing of this book.

I would like to thank my wife Dr. Zehra Rizvi for her unwavering support in bringing this book to fruition. Even with her busy schedule, she managed to provide me her feedback throughout the development process of this book.

My son Dr. Asghar Rizvi and my daughter-in-law Fizza Rizvi were actively involved throughout this project.

I would like to thank Ms. Reese Norton of AuthorHouse for helping me through the publication process.

# Glossary

| | |
|---|---|
| Aaley | Progeny |
| Abbasids | Abbasid dynasty from the line of Ibn Abbas Muhammad's paternal uncle. |
| Abrahamic religions | Judaism, Christianity and Islam. Religions originating from the lineage of Prophet Abraham. |
| Adahith | Traditions - Prophet Muhammad's sayings, actions, approvals and disapprovals transmitted through reliable authentic narrators. |
| Ahl | People. In general a qualification for receiving the honor of being an "Ahl" (part of a family or household). Chapter 2. |
| Ahl al Bayt | People of a household |
| Ahleka | female equivalent of Ahl – being part of a household |
| Aiysha | Wife of Muhammad and daughter of Abu Bakr |
| Ali | Husband of Fatimah the daughter of The prophet of Islam. Muhammad's cousin and Son in Law. |
| Asiya | Wife of the Pharaoh who raised Moses. |
| Aya | Verse of Quran |
| Da'wat dhu 'l-'Ashira | First call to Islam. Chapter 4, note 3 |

| | |
|---|---|
| Eisa | Jesus the prophet |
| Fatimah | Daughter of the prophet of Islam Muhammad |
| Hadith | Tradition |
| Hafza | Wife of Muhammad and Daughter of Umar |
| Haqq | Truth. Deeper meaning discussed in the introduction. |
| Hasan | Son of Fatimah and grandson of the Prophet of Islam Muhammad |
| Hazrat | Honorable, Your honor, Sir, respectable |
| Husayn | Son of Fatimah and grandson of the prophet of Islam Muhammad |
| Jamal | Battle between Ali and Aiysha |
| Jibrail | Gabrial – the angel who brought the |
| Kaabah | The holiest site in Islam. The believers face towards Kaabah during the prayers |
| Khadija | First wife of Muhammad and the first one to accept Islam |
| Khandaq | Battle of the Trench. The battle between the forces of Muhammad and Abu Sufyan. |
| Khawarjit | A group who broke off from Islam in opposition to Ali. |
| Lut | A prophet in the lineage of Abraham |

| | |
|---|---|
| Masoom | The concept of a Masoom is that he or she does not under any circumstance commit any sin even though he or she is able to. See under Notes: note 1 chapter 7 |
| Maududi | A scholar and a commentator on Islam |
| Maula | Master, guardian, commander. Chapter 4. |
| Muawiyah | The first dictator who started a Dynasty |
| Mufaser | Interpreter of the verses of Quran - exegete |
| Mufasereen | Plural of Mufaser (interpreters) |
| Muhadith | Narator of traditions |
| Muhaditheen | Plural of Muhadith |
| Muhammad | The prophet of Islam |
| Musa | The prophet who brought the Torah |
| Nuh | A prophet before Abraham |
| S | Salamulaah (peace be upon) |
| SA | Salamullah Alaiha or Salaamullah Alayha (peace be upon her) |
| Safiyya | Wife of Muhammad |
| Sahih | Collection of trackable traditions |
| Sarah | Wife of prophet Abraham |
| SAW | Sallalah alaihay wa Alehi same as SAWS |

| | |
|---|---|
| SAWS | Salalahu aliha wa alehi wa sallam (God bless him and grant him salvation) |
| Sunnah | Actions and sayings of Muhammad (the praxises) transmitted through a chain of reliable narrators. |
| Tafaseer | Collective presentation of interpretations of the verses of Quran |
| Tafseer | Interpretation of the verse of Quran |
| Tawheed | the belief in one God. The concept of singularity of a creator of the universe unique to Islam |
| Umm Salama | Wife of Muhammad |
| Ummayah | The dynasty of Abu Sufyan |
| Zulaiqua | The wife of Aziz |

# Index

## A

Aiysha 15, 16, 17, 18, 19, 21, 22, 24, 26, 37, 64, 68, 89, 90

Ali iii, vii, ix, x, xi, xii, xv, xvi, 1, 2, 9, 14, 15, 16, 17, 18, 19, 20, 21, 22, 23, 24, 25, 26, 27, 28, 29, 30, 31, 32, 33, 34, 35, 36, 38, 44, 49, 55, 56, 59, 60, 62, 63, 64, 65, 66, 67, 70, 71, 72, 73, 74, 75, 76, 77, 78, 79, 82, 86, 88, 89, 90

anfusana 31, 70

Asiya 13, 16, 89

Aya Muwaddah 32, 36, 37

## D

Da'wat dhu 'l-'Ashira 34, 76, 89

## E

Eisa iii, 90

## F

Fatimah iii, ix, x, xi, xvi, 16, 17, 18, 19, 20, 21, 22, 23, 24, 25, 26, 27, 28, 29, 30, 31, 32, 44, 56, 59, 62, 63, 64, 65, 66, 67, 82, 83, 89, 90

## G

Gabriel 15, 67

Ghadir e Khumm 29, 34, 35, 36, 37, 71, 72, 73, 74

9 781728 307510